WRT 1912

CAMBRIDGE

Treasured Perennials

GRAHAM STUART THOMAS, OBE, VMH, DHM, VMM
Gardens Consultant to the National Trust

Preface by Christopher Brickell, CBE, VMH

Foreword by George Waters

A Ngaere Macray Book

SAGAPRESS, INC.
Sagaponack, New York

Copyright 1999 Sagapress, Inc., Sagaponack, NY
All rights reserved

Printed in Hong Kong

Distributed by Timber Press, Portland, Oregon

LIBRARY OF CONGRESS CATALOGING-IN-PUBLICATION DATA

Thomas, Graham Stuart.
    Treasured perennials / Graham Stuart Thomas : preface by
Christopher Brickell ; foreword by George Waters.
       p.   cm.
    "A Ngaere Macray book."
    Includes index.
    ISBN 0-89831-076-8 (hardcover)
    1. Perennials.   I. Title.
SB434.T488   1999
635.9′32—dc21   98-46091
                                          CIP

Endpapers: Drawing of a street in Cambridge by the author's father, 1912.

Opening: A motif which has appeared in all my books, from my original pen-and-ink drawing, here brought to life in silk embroidery by my old friend Beryl Daborn. For this fine gesture she has earned my gratitude.

Frontispiece: A drawing of *Campanula vidalii*, a plant at Knightshayes Court, Devon. This species is a native of the Azores and does not survive cold winters in Britain. It has a woody rootstock and clammy leaves and stem. Flowering in late summer, the white bells have a ring of yellow in the centre. Introduced in 1851, it appreciates stony well drained soil in full sun. From a pencil sketch by the author.

CONTENTS

PREFACE   VII

FOREWORD   IX

INTRODUCTION   XI

PART ONE   Hardy Ferns   I

PART TWO   The Dicots   9

PART THREE   Hardy Grasses   83

PART FOUR   The Monocots   91

PART FIVE   Hardy Orchids   139

PART SIX   Music as an Accompaniment to Flowers
Three poems by A. E. Housman, set to music
for high voice and piano by the Author   143

ENVOI   157

GENERAL INDEX   159

INDEX OF PLANTS   161

PHOTO CREDITS   167

PLANT HARDINESS ZONES IN THE UNITED STATES   168

Gardeners world-wide will be delighted that yet another very fine offering from the eminent pen of Graham Stuart Thomas is available to add to the many well-thumbed, and equally treasured gardening books that have already given, and continue to provide, so much pleasure and good gardening to his many readers.

I first met Graham over forty years ago when I was appointed as assistant to the botanist at Wisley, where he was a frequent and most welcome visitor, travelling over from his home nearby, then at West End near Woking. Prior to that I had perused eagerly his admirable horticultural booklets *The Manual of Shrub Roses* (and its predecessor in 1948, *Roses as Flowering Shrubs*, issued by T. Hilling and Co. of Chobham where he was nursery manager) and *The Modern Florilegium*, slim but extremely informative volumes I still use to this day. Very readable, enjoyable and stimulating too. Where else would you find such evocative descriptions of a plant having a fragrance of "a rich and satisfying odour of hot stewed plums and apricots"—this in reference to *Iris graminea*; or, of *Baptisia australis*, "after the first hard frost the leaves turn coal-black, and are useful for indoor decoration among dried leaves etc." Read any of Graham's books and one finds they are superbly crafted and written with meticulous attention to detail, clearly a result of long personal and practical experience and critical observation.

Although at one time he was considered mainly a specialist rosarian, it is evident from the wealth of G.S.T. publications that the breadth and depth of his horticultural knowledge is spread much more widely. I cannot recall any hardy ornamentals, apart from water plants, that have not come within the scope of his fluent and erudite pen. As a result he has, over the years, been largely responsible for the development of a new generation of thought on the use of plants in garden design—a protagonist of the importance and value of foliage, a revitaliser of interest in "old roses" and a strong exponent of the use of ornamental ground cover, not only to save labour, but to enhance difficult, dull and forgotten areas of gardens. His books, *The Art of Planting* and *Trees in the Landscape*, exemplify well his influence on gardens and garden design, and, as Gardens Adviser and later Gardens Consultant to the National Trust, his expertise has been used to excellent effect in numerous historically important properties including Claremont, Mottisfont, Hidcote and Shugborough.

His fascination with plants of all types dates from the early age of six (four, if one concludes that a photograph of the young G.S.T. with a wheelbarrow was the start of his career!) and this passion has never left him.

But what of the man? My first meeting with Graham was in the staff "tea-room" at Wisley and initially he appeared somewhat austere. It was not long, however, before his underlying sense of fun and an unexpectedly wicked sense of humour came through. I particularly recall during a visit to Stourhead in 1958 or 1959 with Graham and Frank Knight, then Director of Wisley, that the evening at a nearby hotel was much enlivened by an exchange of reminiscences and stories (sometimes risqué!) between them.

During subsequent years of our friendship we have visited many gardens together, a constant and pleasurable learning process for my part, as Graham's vast knowledge of plants, their behaviour and attributes is always made freely available. This characteristic generosity has been of great benefit to many students from Wisley and elsewhere, visits to his garden being much prized and enjoyed—as are the plants distributed as freely as his knowledge.

Music—classical, choral and madrigals—as well as poetry, also figure prominently in Graham's life as will be evident to readers of *Treasured Perennials*, who will find apt verses from A. E. Housman heading each chapter as well as, perhaps unique in a book on gardening, a final section on music as an accompaniment to flowers.

A man of many parts, Graham Thomas's great gardening and writing attributes are interwoven with many other skills—a watercolourist of note, a fine photographer and a diligent historian of matters horticultural.

Blessed with a degree of scholarship given to few, Graham combines practical expertise with artistic flair, botanical accuracy and historical knowledge to provide a contribution to horticulture I believe is scarcely paralleled this century.

The measure of Graham Stuart Thomas, now in his ninety-first year, is his continued industry. Bending to weed in his garden among his beloved plants may now be difficult but, as will be found by readers of *Treasured Perennials*, his horticultural cornucopia still spills over generously—to the benefit of all gardeners.

Christopher Brickell, CBE, VMH
West Sussex, England

Of the many books on gardens and gardening that line my shelves, most are valued references; only a handful are there for the sheer pleasure of reading. Among that precious few is Graham Thomas's *The Rock Garden and its Plants*, an entertaining and informative discussion on every aspect of its subject from palaeogeology to alpine plants. We have come to expect this broad view in Mr Thomas's books: his *Trees in the Landscape*, a revised edition of which appeared in 1997, shows the influence of trees on the beauty of natural and man-made landscapes, providing *en passant* a critique of our destruction of the former and attempts at enhancing the latter; his writing on roses, now available in one volume as *The Graham Stuart Thomas Rose Book*, surveys these most popular of plants, wild and cultivated, ancient and modern, showing their value to the gardener with reference to literature, history, and horticulture. Even in *Plants for Ground Cover* a mundane subject is enlivened with carefully observed descriptions of naturally occurring ecosystems, including heathland, beech woods, chalk hills, and the marshy borders of estuaries. These examples, encouraging us towards a sounder, less chemical way of gardening, were, I must add, offered in 1970.

And throughout his ever growing body of work is evidence not only of a profound knowledge of plants and gardening, but also of a passion for poetry and music, and great skill as a watercolorist. It is his all-embracing view that holds my attention and gives me pleasure in reading that few others writing on gardening can provide.

From what better gardener than Graham Thomas then, could we ask a list of favorite perennials? Aimed at others, the request would be irrelevant: a publisher had better ask for "the hundred best," or something like that, in hope of deceiving purchasers with the promise of universality among plants. But Mr Thomas's broad experience and dogged unconformity lift him out of the ordinary: his list of favorites may never be ours, but inquisitive gardeners feel a need for it; knowledge of it has value, and the reading will delight.

At every page of *Treasured Perennials* I am reminded of the manuals written by Mr Thomas for Sunningdale Nursery which, with James Russell, he managed for some years in the 1960s. In them I found an extraordinary range of plants rarely mentioned in other books on gardening. These plants were chosen mainly for their foliage and suggested for display in unusual combinations. The nursery was, clearly, a place I should see. To give myself time for thorough exploration I bicycled down the A30, then a main road from London to the West Country, through Staines and Egham to Sunningdale, and pitched a small tent in a field opposite the nursery. From this encampment sorties were made to admire and select from the nursery's magnificent double borders of mostly herbaceous perennials. I found a wonderland of hellebores and hostas, ligularias and lavenders, miscanthus and matteuccia, salvias and saxifrages. It was without doubt, "the most beautiful and interesting nursery in the country," as claimed in those manuals.

So, here is Mr Thomas's personal choice offered to gardeners in the '90s, generously illustrated and handsomely bound. Here are the surprising and illuminating references to palaeontology and geology; the recollections of great gardeners whose plants these were; the tips on cultivation from seventy years' experience, commercial, private, and in the service of the nation. And here are plants: the prevalent and the rare; the ancient survivals and the newly minted. Mr Thomas's selections have little regard for the currently fashionable, but have impressed him with their extraordinary beauty, history, or utility. Some of them will affect you in a similar way.

George Waters
Berkeley, California

When green buds hang in the elm like dust
  And sprinkle the lime like rain,
Forth I wander, forth I must,
  And drink of life again.

Forth I must by hedgerow bowers
  To look at the leaves uncurled,
And stand in fields where cuckoo-flowers
  Are lying about the world.

More Poems, ix, by A. E. Housman

There is no doubt that it was of real and lasting benefit to have been born in Cambridge. There was the charm of the old city—or town as it then was: its greens and open spaces; the rivulets down the main streets; a Castle Hill, though without a castle; its several ancient churches; a small river, the Cam, winding its way slowly to the Wash and the North Sea; and the great assembly of university buildings crowned with the superb edifice of the 16th century chapel of King's College. Apart from weekly services, great music was performed in the chapel from time to time; likewise in the Guildhall on Market Hill. This "hill" was strangely a level area, but any slight eminence was called a hill in flat Cambridgeshire. There was also the renowned University Botanic Garden dating from 1836 which, in spite of a rather heavy limy soil contained a noteworthy collection of trees, shrubs and plants, with representatives from all over the world, set in a fine design. And then, of course, there were the museums, some containing rocks, fossils, and skeletons, and one devoted to great works of art.

But above all there was the magnificence of the college buildings, enough to inspire any youngster to become an architect. The opportunity was there; one of my godfathers was an architect practising in the town. (He was incidentally a keen and knowledgeable gardener.) He, unfortunately, died while I was quite young. Though his theories and expertise of architecture were thus denied me, the fascination of stone and rocks never left me. Each college has its own chapel and I saw the great contrast between the mellowed Yorkshire stone of the chapels and the rather harsh white Portland stone from Dorset of neighbouring buildings.

In general I think it has been religion in one form or another that has inspired mankind to erect the largest and most beautiful buildings, from the bald and unwieldly monoliths of Stonehenge to the latest cathedrals.

In the botanic garden was a rock garden of brown Hornton stone from Oxfordshire. Another, at Sidney Sussex College, was of grey limestone from Derbyshire. These were unusual, and caught my attention as at that time, in the early years of the 20th century, the beautiful waterworn limestone from Westmorland was being used for many rock gardens throughout the country because of its weathered beauty. The carting away of thousands of tons of this beautiful stone, which lies on the surface of the land and cannot be quarried, has led to great despoilation and the owners are now putting a stop to its transportation.

Sadly there was no rock of any kind occurring naturally within cycling distance of my home, only chalk. I say "only" because except in its hardest manifestations, known as clunch, it is too soft for building. Old walls of clunch are still to be seen here and there throughout the chalk country, with a capping of tiles or even thatch. From time immemorial, chalk and its hard version, limestone, have been of inestimable use in building, for they contribute cement to the mortar with which brick, stone, and concrete blocks are held together. In addition, chalk and limestone have been quarried by the million tons for hundreds of years and spread over farming lands to increase fertility.

Our annual family holidays were spent on the Norfolk coast, being the nearest part of the country to Cambridge where a fresh sea-breeze could be enjoyed. Because of its surrounding arable land Cambridge tends to be cold in winter and hot in summer. Much of Norfolk is flat and likewise farmed, but in the north-east corner of the county there is a dramatic change. The high ground beginning with the Chiltern Hills nearly at the middle of England and stretching eastward across the country peters out in a short range of cliffs abruptly facing the sea at Hunstanton.

Within a short walk of the cliffs is a sandy salt-marsh, home to many unusual plants that can put up with occasional flooding by the sea. It was enough to whet the appetite of any young gardener, especially one who already had a leaning towards rock gardening and diminutive plants.

Despite my deep interest in rock in one form or another, and all its uses, our annual holidays remained in East Anglia for many years until, goaded by pictures of Cotswold towns and villages and their splendid architecture, our steps were eventually turned west towards Stow-on-the-Wold, in Gloucestershire. Here and in the villages around were enough buildings to enchant me. Not the least attraction was the steep tilt of the roofs and gables occasioned by the weight of the heavy, splitstone tiles. Moreover there were quarries where the building stone was extracted. Even the local flora was different, in fact, unique.

Meanwhile my interest in stone for rock gardens was whetted by my first visit to Chelsea Flower Show, the annual spectacle organised by the Royal Horticultural Society. Here was my first sight of great rock gardens.

Near at home was a firm of stone-masons whose friendly employees gave me any small pieces of stone that took my eye. Among the pieces were slabs of coarse limestone, which I took for the tiny fossils of marine life contained in them. And by great good luck a consignment of Derbyshire limestone was delivered outside a large house nearby, to be used in the construction of a rock garden. Among the lumps I spotted the form of an ammonite, a species of shell-fish now extinct, exposed to full view. That piece of rock also found a place in the small patch I called my garden.

Much the same happened when an inferior consignment of coal was delivered to my parents' home. Good coal was shiny and often of light weight but this load was heavy and slatey; the kind that when burnt gives little heat and turns to white dust. Some lumps had the unmistakeable marks of the bark of *Sigillaria*, one of the giant clubmosses which, among other growths, went to make what we call today the coal measures. You may rest assured that at least one of these fossil-marked pieces did not go into the grate.

This was all brought home to me by a piece of great good fortune. During the two or three years when I was learning the rudiments of gardening at the University Botanic Garden it so happened that a series of lectures, given every winter in the Cambridge Public Library, was focussed in 1927–8 on the geological history and evolution of the plant world. Of course I attended the lectures and was interested to find that two scientists of some standing in the university were also attending. They were Dr C. C. Hurst, whose work was, in after years, such an influence in my researches into the genus *Rosa*, and Miss Saunders, whose experiments in plant breeding were nursed from seeds to infancy and fruition in the botanic garden. There were other dignitaries present but the fog of time obscures them from my memory.

A. C. Seward, Master of Downing College and Professor of Botany in the University, was the lecturer. He was concise, direct, and had a prodigious memory and clear enunciation. (I had previously attended his year of lectures on elementary botany.) Many of the other lecturers that I heard had not half his gifts; there was no difficulty in making notes, which I still have.

All these occurrences had a considerable effect on my outlook and influenced my thoughts about gardening. This book owes much to these early observations and instructions. In addition I have followed another enthusiasm of my early years in bringing the verse of A. E. Housman (1859–1936) to the fore in these chapters. Hence the few lines at the head of each chapter. Housman had to me an almost uncanny skill of wringing the utmost meaning and impact, not from convoluted and extravagant phrasing, but from simple, often short, words. They ring truer today than the breathy, multitudinous words which go to make up what is nowadays called poetry.

When, on moving to Surrey, I became more earnest about music and joined with friends to form a choral group, it was Housman who inspired my few tentative efforts at composition. Those of my readers who share that enthusiasm and wish to study my settings of Houseman's verse are invited to turn to Part Six, where words and music are reproduced.

This book is simply the outcome of a desire to give some lesser known plants publicity, to bring forward some gems of the past and to act as a fanfare for a few newer plants. We start off with ferns because they are an ancient, historic class of plants, and then we find ourselves at the dividing of the ways. All other herbaceous perennials, and indeed all other flowering plants, are classified by the learned botanists as either Dicotyledonous or Monocotyledonous. These two rather cumbersome names are not mystifying nor difficult; they simply intimate that all flowering plants when raised from seed have either two seed leaves or only one. We all know what mustard and cress look like when young, and anyone who has raised marrows or cucumbers will not be likely to forget the pair of broad leaves that first show above ground. These Dicotyledonous plants almost invariably have the veins of the leaf crossing and joining into a net pattern and are thus known also as net-veined leaves. This is what we learnt at our preparatory school. There are other special characters, connected with the flowers rather than the leaves, that need not concern us here.

On the other hand, the second great group, the Monocotyledonous plants, have only one cotyledon or first seed leaf. Most bulbous plants have this characteristic, also grasses, including bamboos. Moreover, the leaves of this group are usually what is known as entire—not divided or lobed. We can readily call to mind daffodils and tulips, *Kniphofia* and the various arums and aroids. Thus they give quite a different "line" and deportment in the garden and have a soothing effect on the senses as opposed to the Dicots (as they are usually called, with Monocots for the second group).

The Dicots contain such disparate genera as *Delphinium, Acanthus,* and *Anemone,* all distinguished by the pair of seed leaves that is their hallmark. It will be obvious to gardeners how enriched are our garden landscapes with these two widely differing styles of foliage.

This is, I think, enough of introductory matter to enable us to grasp the immense range of foliage alone among plants I am about to describe. So come with me and look through the plates and paragraphs; we will start with the ferns and then the Dicots and move on to the grasses (these being wind pollinated) and to the other Monocots, finishing with a few choice hardy orchids which have perhaps the most involved cooperation between flower and insect. We will treat the plants within each group alphabetically by genus.

Treasured Perennials

Dryopteris affinis (*D. pseudomas*)

PART ONE

Hardy Ferns

Star and coronal and bell
April underfoot renews,
And the hope of man as well
Flowers among the morning dews.

Last Poems, XVI, by A. E. Housman

I t is usual when writing about hardy plants to relegate ferns to the concluding chapters. However this book is an exception. I have deliberately placed the ferns at the beginning because they have an ancient history and in the world's flora are related to ferns prevalent in the carboniferous period, when the coal seams were being formed. While ferns have an undoubted and unique beauty they cannot be said to compete with our more obvious flowering plants. Nevertheless gardens would be much poorer without them. Who has not been captivated by the delicate tints of unfurling fronds of ferns in wood or garden—or for that matter on our western shores and islands, wherever there is coolth to be enjoyed? And as in nature, they stand supreme in their lacy filigree; it is just this character that makes them so valued in gardens, and their long-lasting beauty stays to act as a foil to more brilliant plants. I do not think I could make a garden without using the beauty of ferns somewhere.

In the fern world, what we are looking at and appreciating is not the whole plant; the real plant, with a sex life all its own, is a little thing like a liverwort called a prothallus. It develops on the soil surface from a spore fallen from a fern frond. When mature the prothallus releases sperm that wanders off if the soil is moist in search of a mate. It may fertilize its own or another prothallus, but in either case it puts down roots and throws up growth completely dwarfing the prothallus; this is what we know as the fern in nature and in our gardens. It is analogous in its way to the mushroom and other fungi that appear above ground only when their questing underground threads (perhaps the "black bootlaces" of our dreaded honey fungus) unite and produce the toadstools which we know so well. Both toadstools and ferns are there to provide the spores to start a new life-cycle. Hybrids among either are rare but do occur among ferns, and start life from the liverwort-like growth of the prothallus.

So that in ferns as we see them we are contemplating the ultimate growth of the fern-cycle, bent specially towards the production of infinitesimal numbers of spores which drop, or are blown about by the wind when ripe; the majority of them perish, but on cool moist surfaces in woodland, cliffs or the bases of hedgerows they take hold, grow and mate to start the cycle over again.

Spores of most ferns start life on the lower surfaces of fronds tucked under a tiny cover or flap known as the shield or indusium. (One fern on which the covers are prominent is known as the Shield Fern.) To raise ferns from spores the whole frond should be cut at the right moment and laid face uppermost on moist peat in a box or pan, sprayed with water, covered with a sheet of glass or polythene, placed in the shade and left alone. Those who are specially conscious of the environment may look askance at my recommendation of peat, but this commodity is more likely to be free of weed seeds, and spores from unwanted ferns, than the choicest leaf mould. After a few weeks the surface of the peat will be covered with tiny green moss-like growths, some of which will eventually become the ferns desired. If they germinate well you will have far more than you want. Fern species mature at different times in the summer and a lot depends on watching the progress of the spores under their little lids, and when they mature, on handling the frond gently when cutting so as not to shake out the spores before placing it on the peat.

Some ferns in moist west-country gardens germinate freely on mossy banks, even in grass. At Glendurgan, Cornwall, the tree ferns (*Dicksonia*) spring up voluntarily on mossy banks and path verges in the sheltered valley.

Although the majority of ferns have their young spores attached to the backs of the fronds, in plants of several genera and species they are carried on the tops of the stems, as in *Osmunda regalis*, or on special stems alone, as in *Matteuccia*, *Blechnum* and a few others. In the former genus the fruiting stems stay aloft long after the foliage has died down.

The delicate fronds of Maidenhair Fern have decorated many a dainty corsage. It grows wild in a rocky promontory in Lancashire, also in Ireland, within close reach of the sea. But it is not generally hardy in the British Isles, being usually grown in greenhouses. We are fortunate in having two close relatives that are totally hardy. One, the little creeping *Adiantum venustum*, which I find a perfect foil for hardy cyclamens, is only about four inches high. The other is *A. pedatum*, a native of many temperate countries including North America, the Aleutian Islands and Japan. Its wiry black stems support a most elegantly shaped fan of pinnae. In spring it is delicate green, assuming darker tones as the

Adiantum pedatum

season advances. From Japan we have a form, *A. pedatum* 'Japonicum', whose young fronds in spring are warm rosy brown or copper-coloured, while from the Aleutians comes a dwarf form of distinctly glaucous hue, called *A. pedatum subpumilum* (erroneously called 'Aleuticum'). This has a low-growing stem, only a few inches tall, whereas the others may reach a foot.

All these ferns are easy to cultivate in any friable soil to which plenty of compost or leaf mould has been added. Limy soil is quite acceptable to all ferns save *Blechnum* and *Cryptogamma*.

We have one native of Britain and indeed of many other parts of the Old World, *Dryopteris pseudomas* (*D. borreri*), which takes some beating if you leave out the Royal Fern. I have seen scores of this majestic plant on the west coast of Scotland, and isolated groups of it in Cornwall and elsewhere. In late spring it is readily picked out at a distance by the unique tint of the young fronds; they are upstanding to four feet and distinctly yellowish green. The stems are covered with long hairy brownish scales and the pinnae are regular. It is far more beautiful and imposing than the similar common Male Fern that we meet

Dryopteris wallichiana

Matteuccia orientalis

in every garden. *D. pseudomas* is given full importance in the lily wood at Mount Stewart, Northern Ireland, where the clumps reach almost to six feet.

This beautiful species has a close relative in eastern countries, from the Himalaya to Japan: *Dryopteris wallichiana*. It has all the good points of *D. pseudomas*, but its splendid fronds of the same yellowish green in spring are most strikingly contrasted by sepia hairs and scales on the stems. While it grows quite well for me in my garden, I have known it suffer in severe winters, so in cold districts I recommend giving it a covering of old fern fronds in addition to its own. It is worth the extra care; a well grown clump may top four feet and can be the most compelling of all greenery. Although there is a superficial resemblance between these two species and the common Male Fern, their decisive horizontal pinnae score heavily over all others.

While the Ostrich Plume Fern, *Matteuccia struthiopteris* (*Struthiopteris germanica*) is fairly well known, and colonizes many a damp garden with its spreading roots, it has a failing in that in late summer or early autumn it fades and dies down, leaving the short fertile fronds standing erect for the whole winter. Less known and grown is *M. orientalis*; its arching fronds, both fertile and sterile, mark it apart from *M. struthiopteris*. In addition its sterile fronds turn to lovely amber-yellow in late autumn. It also appreciates damp ground and, as its name suggests, is a native of the Far East. It achieves about two feet in height and width.

There is no doubt that apart from tree ferns, which are hardy only in our most sheltered coombs in Cornwall and western Scotland, the Royal Fern, *Osmunda regalis*, has pride of place. It can grow to six feet tall, making a huge woody base clothed in brown moss-like roots. Age-old clumps may be several feet across at ground level. There is room for it only at the side of large ponds and lakes, but fortunately there is a much smaller

Osmunda cinnamomea

Polystichum polyblepharum

Polystichum munitum

form called 'Gracilis' which is seldom more than three feet tall. This grows well on the stream-fed rock garden at Sizergh Castle, Cumberland, and is a charming plant to be greatly treasured. It is unaccountably rare, but used to seed itself on moist, mossy sandstone rocks in my garden and should be easy to multiply commercially. Also at Sizergh Castle is *O. regalis* 'Purpurascens' whose young and immature fronds are tinted glaucous purple. When I moved house some twenty-five years ago I gave all these osmundas to the Royal Horticultural Society garden at Wisley and they appreciated the moisture and shelter of the woodland, and I believe are still there. There is a crested form, *O. regalis* 'Cristata', but it has no attraction for me. Two quite distinct species are *O. claytoniana*, whose spores are borne on separate lobes in the middle of the frond, and *O. cinnamomea* in which they are borne on separate stems. While these two are natives of North America, *O. regalis* occurs all round the world, both north and south—a true relic of bygone ages.

There are two so-called Sword Ferns in North America, one from the eastern states, *Polystichum acrostichoides*, and one from the west, *P. munitum*. Both are also known as Christmas Fern on account of their winter-proof, dark green fronds. The pinnae are not divided into lobes, merely serrate, and of shining dark green. The second species has its spores limited to the uppermost pinnae, which are reduced in size, giving the sword a point, as it were. Both species bear their spores on the backs of the fronds. I had *P. munitum* growing at one time with hellebores and the winter contrast gave me great satisfaction.

An even more distinctively shining evergreen is *Polystichum squarrosum*. The fronds are quite hard to the touch. I have had it only a short while, but it has not suffered in the winter. Its home is the Far East. I take a special delight in late spring (most ferns wake up rather late) in watching the unfurling of the fronds of *P. polyblepharum*. The pinnae seem both to open out and gather together for some days, even weeks, at the tip of the fronds, forming an incurved point. It is a real treasure of shining dark green but only partially evergreen.

Aster × frikartii

PART TWO

The Dicots

Oh see how thick the goldcup flowers
Are lying in field and lane,
With dandelions to tell the hours
That never are told again.

A Shropshire Lad, v, A. E. Housman

Acanthus mollis and *A. spinosus* are two well known old garden plants, invasive but highly decorative, thriving in well drained soil in sunny positions. A third, *A. dioscoridis*, is no exception, though I have not known it to be invasive. It is a native of the Middle East and India, but a plant at Beech Park, near Dublin, of a form that used to be called *A. perringii*, comes from Asia Minor. Its leaves, like those of most acanthuses, are deeply divided and the flowers owe their clear pink tint to the single lip that is the floral attraction of all species. It has been grown in our gardens for about a hundred years, whereas *A. spinosus* from southern Europe has been known for considerably longer.

Acanthus spinosus is perhaps the most imposing of all the species. The leaves are supposed to have provided inspiration for the decoration on capitals of Corinthian columns. We are lucky that Lady Moore, revered Irish gardener, cherished the form that bears her name; its leaves are spectacular in spring, being nearly white from infinitesimal spotting and becoming green later. Lady Moore's plant does not flower freely, its spring foliage being the main attraction. Its invasive, clump-forming habit is valuable where a mass of dense greenery is needed. The acanthuses are not reliably hardy in cold districts.

Because of their early growth in spring, aconitums should only be divided or planted in autumn. They have poisonous tuberous roots, in appearance not unlike those of the Jerusalem Artichoke with which they have sometimes been fatally confused. They are among the most ornamental genera of Ranunculaceae in their deeply laciniate foliage.

Acanthus spinosus 'Lady Moore'   *Aconitum napellus* 'Album Grandiflorum'

Aconitum napellus is the Monkshood of wide distribution in Europe and Asia and has been cultivated for centuries. The flowers, like those of so many of the species, are of dark lavender-tinted blue, but there are rare variants, notably 'Album Grandiflorum' and 'Carneum'. The former is sumptuous creamy white, a colour that enlivens any grouping of flowers. 'Carneum' in Scottish gardens has flowers of soft flesh-pink, but in the warmer, drier south of Britain they lose colour quickly and become dirty white. Neither of them is common in our gardens but both are well worth searching for. The stamens and the tiny petals at the centres of flowers in all species are short, but the stigmas are curved to fit into the top sepal or hood (so aptly described by Monkshood), a device ensuring that some pollen reaches its appointed place on the backs of visiting insects.

The Baneberries are known botanically as *Actaea*, and there is a beautiful white *Narcissus* named 'Actaea'. I always thought the name commemorated a nymph or goddess, but no, it is simply the Greek name for Elder (*Sambucus*). The actaeas of our gardens resemble elders in their leaves, which are lobed like those of an elder. (The leaves of all elders are thus divided and most bear red or black berries—the result of the fluffy white flowers getting pollinated.) Also like the elder, the berries of *Actaea spicata* are dark red or black, on a plant about two feet high. It is often called Herb Christopher, but the connection is difficult to see; is it because the flowers and berries are carried aloft as St Christopher carried the infant Christ over the river? But *A. alba*, as its name suggests, not only has white flowers (like all the others) but white berries too. This fact would not make it a conspicuous garden plant, but towards the autumn when the leaves are yellowing and the berries

Aconitum napellus 'Carneum'

Anemone × hybrida 'Honorine Jobert'   *Anemone hupehensis* var. *japonica*

(poisonous) are becoming white their stalks thicken and turn to scarlet. Truly a remarkable plant, well displayed in the woodland garden at Knightshayes Court, Devon.

There is to me always a note of sadness when the Japanese anemones start to flower; usually it is August but may be as early as the last weeks of July in forward seasons. It is the foretaste of autumn: with the phloxes all the excitement of the early year is gone. But we should take courage; August and September will see clump after clump of magnificent anemones in flower. And not only in flower, but poised over handsome foliage that has been in beauty since spring and will carry on past flowering time until autumn tints the leaves. I have a garden seat near a group of *Anemone × hybrida* 'Honorine Jobert' and I never sit there without contemplating with enormous enjoyment the beauty of the sculptured, silky white flowers with their circle of yellow stamens around the bright green centre. I think there is no doubt that this plant is the most beautiful of all the Japanese anemones, though it arose at Verdun about 1858, a white sport of the almost-as-beautiful pink *A. × hybrida*, a cross raised about 1847. The parents were *A. vitifolia*, from Upper Burma, and a variety, long known in the Far East, *A. hupehensis japonica*. Many subsequent hybrids have been raised and named in England and mainland Europe, but in my opinion not one is so beautiful as these two original near-singles, despite larger flowers and double the number of segments in some of them.

This original wild hybrid, if it may so be called, *Anemone hupehensis japonica*, has been in cultivation for a long time and by some mischance became confused with 'Prinz Heinrich' ('Prince Henry'). It has been a fertile parent and prolific spreader, suggesting to me that in these Japanese anemones we have the ideal naturalising plants: their wandering rootstocks will take command of any cool or sunny meadow where early bulbs provide the overture.

The Japanese anemones and other tall growers do not take kindly to transplanting unless the finer surface-wandering roots are chosen. The coarser black thong-like roots are not so successful. Though they are as a group often recommended for shade, in my experience Japanese anemones flower most freely in sunny places; at the same time I must mention that a cool retentive soil such as may sometimes be found near a north facing wall suits them best, but preferably not under tree-shade, though they will thrive even in such untoward conditions. Late autumn or winter is the best time for transplanting: they get into growth rather early in spring—in fact they have a long working life.

One of the prettiest sights in our woods and in our gardens is provided by the early spring display of the Wood Anemone, *Anemone nemorosa*. It is a small plant, seldom exceeding six inches except in very good soil in shade. When fully established it spreads freely by means of a wandering rootstock and by seed. To me there are few spring flowers so winsome and lasting. They are mostly white, often flushed with pink on the reverse, the flowers held just above the neatly divided leaves. There are many named variants, 'Lismore Pink' being delicately tinted with pink on the face as well as on the reverse. Others are richly rosy on the reverse, white within. The double 'Vestal', whose stamens have turned into petals making a fine tuft in the centre, is historic. I have another kind in which the central shortest segments turn blue when the flower is fully expanded. These and others grow in the National Anemone Collection at Knightshayes Court, Devon.

Much like *Anemone nemorosa* in growth is *A. ranunculoides*. While the former is a native

Anemone nemorosa 'Vestal'

Anemone narcissiflora

of Britain and other parts of Europe, the latter is only found in central and eastern Europe and, as can be seen from a visit to the garden at Hidcote, Gloucestershire, where it grows, has flowers of bright yellow. I have a plant whose flowers are double and last even longer than the several weeks of these two species. Hybrids between the two, named *A.* × *seemannii* (*A.* × *lipsiensis*), have pale yellow flowers and on the best of these the flowers are wider than usual; these should be sought. After transplanting they all generally take several seasons to become established sufficiently to colonise the ground. Mice are, unfortunately, partial to the foliage of these small plants, sometimes eating it to the ground. This may kill the plants if it happens two seasons running.

In the spring season the Pasque Flower appears. Botanists have ordained that since the seeds carry long hairy awns these shall be grouped not as anemones but in the genus *Pulsatilla*, and under that name they will be found in this book. But we need not be long without anemones in the garden; one or another of them is in flower through spring and summer. Among the loveliest for June is *Anemone narcissiflora*, a well known plant of the United States, the Alps, and of Europe generally. It is aptly named, for above the tump of divided leaves sheaves of white flowers are borne not unlike a bunch of narcissi. Often the outer segments are flushed with some shade of blue or lilac, a feature more noticeable in its close relative from Asia, *A. rivularis*. Both should be established from pots and left severely alone where they thrive.

The ivy family has some surprises for us gardeners: Araliaceae includes not only the ivies but giant shrubs (*Aralia* and *Fatsia*) in addition to a few herbaceous aralias, of which *Aralia racemosa* is one. It is a North American native known since the 17th century but never widely grown in gardens. Although hardy, it is not of great floristic charm; however its rounded heads of small white flowers are borne on branching spikes each one of which resembles a head of ivy blooms. The stems are usually dark brown and the foliage hand-

Aralia racemosa

somely divided. In all it is a statuesque plant to lend enchantment to a garden brimming over with flowers.

When considering the artemisias we start off with a mystery: nobody knows exactly the origin or parentage of *Artemisia* 'Powis Castle'. Because it was found by or raised by Mr James Hancock, the highly successful former head gardener at Powis Castle, it has seemed fit to name it in honour of that renowned garden. It was somewhere about 1978 that it first made an appearance and it has proved its worth ever since, being hardy in the south of England, though it may suffer in cold wet winters. It was Margery Fish who selected two silvery leafed forms of the common Wormwood, *A. absinthium*, and I suspect one of these may have been a parent of 'Powis Castle'. It is thought that *A. arborescens*, that silvery leafed, lacy, although by no means hardy paragon, may have been the other. 'Powis Castle' is a low shrubby plant making a dome of fine silvery laciniate leaves, which when fully established may be five feet across, but less than half that in height. It is intelligently used in a bone-dry, sun scorched position, under overspreading yew topiary on one of the terraces at Powis Castle. A more untoward spot could hardly be found; grass never survived there. It scarcely ever flowers but the foliage has in plenty the fragrance of many of these species.

My first sight of *Artemisia vallesiaca* was in Lady Moore's garden at Rathfarnham, near Dublin. There was a large old beech tree in the garden standing on something of a mound with the south and western sun pouring onto the rooty ground. "For such positions I always choose silvery leafed plants" she said. How right she was; they thrive where nothing else would. *A. vallesiaca* was one of them—a neat, extra silvery subshrubby little plant of a foot or so, of strict yet slightly arching growth. All such silvery plants are best planted in spring. It is a native of Switzerland, Italy and Dalmatia, and has long been grown in our gardens alongside the similar *A. canescens*.

Artemisia vallesiaca

Artemisia 'Powis Castle'

"Should be in every garden" is a phrase beloved by over persuasive compilers of catalogues. But can you imagine anything more maddening than to find one's favourite plant repeated in every neighbour's garden? Even so, *Aster × frikartii* would be as worthy as any for such preferential treatment. It has many assets besides undoubted beauty, if you are fortunate enough to acquire the best of them; under this name are offered two or three plants of inferior quality and stance. The best are 'Eiger', 'Jungfrau' and 'Mönch', all named by Frikart of Switzerland. I have had 'Mönch' since the 1920s and have no hesitation in giving it first place; it was awarded the First Class Certificate in recent trials by the Royal Horticultural Society at Wisley, Surrey.

'Mönch' is a slowly increasing clump-forming plant, best propagated by basal cuttings in spring. The leaves are of ordinary aster shape borne freely on self-reliant and branching stems reaching two-to-three feet in height. By late summer they start to produce wide, lavender-blue, yellow centred daisies—a show that continues non-stop until late October. During this long period there are few plants that can hold a candle to it. The special asset of 'Mönch' is the regularity and complete flatness of the array of petals, not equalled by others.

Aster × frikartii is a hybrid between *A. thompsonii* and *A. amellus*. I have never seen the former and I do not think it is in cultivation, though *A. thompsonii* 'Nanus' is fairly well known: a nice little thing usually about one foot in height with rather irregularly rayed flowers produced for a long period. There is no doubt that this species gives *A. × frikartii* its long period of bloom, for *A. amellus* and its many named forms flower for only about a month. Both 'Eiger' and 'Jungfrau', nearer to the amellus parent, are seldom seen.

Among astilbes there are plants with graceful arching plumes of flowers that are better than the more usual upright ones for blending with other plants in the garden. Altogether, the many named varieties provide some of the most vivid colours of the summer months, but they must have moist friable soil. They range from white through pink and mauve to brightest and richest crimson and red. The strong colours are the result of hybridising with *Astilbe davidii*, from China, and three white-flowered astilbes from Japan. The work was begun in 1907 by Messrs Lemoine of Nancy, France, and taken up later by Georg Arends of Ronsdorf, Germany. The desire no doubt was to infuse the white flowers with pink from the Chinese plants, and well did the raisers attain their objective.

The three astilbes from Japan were *A. astilboides*, with erect plumes of horizontal branches; *A. japonica*, whose branches are erect, and *A. thunbergii*, in which the branches are gracefully recurving. To those familiar with these plants it is obvious that the last of these has given elegance to astilbes such as 'Ostrich Plume', 'Betsy Cuperus' and 'Professor van der Wielen'. The last mentioned is the strongest grower. There are many upright-growing sorts in a wide range of colouring, containing the brightest reds. Of late years another Chinese plant has entered the strain, *A. tacquetii*, with dark leaves and narrow upright

Astilbe 'Etna'

Astilbe 'Ostrich Plume'

spikes of rich magenta flowers. It has been the influence in creating late flowering kinds such as 'Jo Ophorst' and 'Purpurlanz'. In all, the astilbes range from two feet in height to four.

Astilbes have many assets for moist gardens. The leaves are much divided, almost fern-like, and many of the dark-flowered sorts have young foliage of the colour of copper beech leaves. When the flowers are over the stems stay aloft, unless overwhelmed by snow, giving a rich brown effect through the winter. After many years the root-crowns tend to rise out of the ground and the flower spikes become smaller. Then is the time to lift the clumps, divide them with a sharp spade, and replant in soil well dug and enriched.

So long as the ground is moist they will do well in sun or part shade. They are often erroneously called spiraeas, some of which they do indeed resemble in their flower plumes, but spiraeas belong to the rose family whereas astilbes are in the saxifrage family.

Baptisia australis is a long-lived plant with deep-questing carrot-like roots, and so when once established in good soil in a sunny spot it should not be disturbed. It is best to start with quite young plants and I fancy they grow best in lime-free soil. They will reach four feet in height with copious blue-green leaves, freely branching and topped with lupin-like spikes of pea flowers in soft, pale, indigo-blue. These develop into handsome dark grey pods and after autumn frost the leaves become completely coal-black. It is easy to raise from seeds, and flowers in early summer, gradually making an ever more impressive annual spectacle. It belongs to the pea family, is a native of eastern North America, and has been known and grown—easily—since 1758. Baptisias yield a blue dye and are known as false indigo in their homeland.

It may seem a little strange to include a begonia in a book concerned with hardy plants but *Begonia grandis* has grown and thrived in my garden without protection, in shade, for several years. It is true that during this period we have had no lengthy spells of severe weather, but the plant produces bulbils which speedily grow to flowering size. Achieving some two feet in shady positions it is a plant of varied colouring. The stems are rich red, likewise the backs of the leaves, which are of the usual lopsided shape of begonias; the upper surfaces of the leaves are sallow green. The flowers are light pink, produced abundantly when summer wanes and the cool nights arrive. I challenge any gardener not to be thrilled with the success of growing this charming plant. It used to be known as *B. evansiana*, and has been grown in our gardens (usually in a cool greenhouse) since 1804. There may be some variation in hardiness depending on the provenance of plants, for it is a native of Malay, China and Japan. But it is easily raised from seed, and it is about time that its general durability and garden merit were understood.

I feel a little diffident about including *Campanula punctata* in these pages for its running roots make it an arrant coloniser of ground. But it is different from most bell flowers in its floral colour. The tubular bells are white or light pink heavily spotted with red inside, and they hang, a few at a time, from foot-high stems. It is the unusual colour and length of flower that earns it a place here. The toothed leaves are nettle-like and make a fairly efficient ground cover, but some might say it is simply substituting one weed for another. It is a native of Siberia and Japan that has been in our gardens a long while, but is enjoying renewed popularity in gardens where novel and choice plants are cosseted, and I fancy it has recently been reintroduced. *C. punctata* is included here also because it is probably a parent of that superlative hybrid *C. × burghaltii*, long treasured and the inspiration for a pencil drawing reproduced in my *Perennial Garden Plants*. *C. punctata* is easy to please in any friable soil, and is best transplanted in early spring in readiness for flowering after midsummer.

Cardamine heptaphylla used to be called *Dentaria pinnata*. Suffice it to say that this is a good garden plant, presenting its pretty heads of snow-white flowers just as the daffodils are passing. It reaches to about eighteen inches from a slowly increasing root; the leaves are pinnate, as its name suggests, with the flowers borne on stems reaching well above them. I have always given it the benefit of shade but I doubt whether it is particular, since it has a short season above ground and dies down early to prepare underground for gladdening our eyes again next spring. It responds well to division after flowering.

It is fortunate that the proposed name, *Dendranthema*, has been dropped so that we can still call our old garden favourites *Chrysanthemum*. This note is concerned with the old

Begonia grandis (B. evansiana)

Cardamine heptaphylla

Campanula punctata

Chrysanthemum 'Emperor of China'

variety 'Emperor of China', established at least as early as 1893 when an exact engraving of its exquisite flowers—crimson in the bud opening to soft pink—appeared in William Robinson's *The English Flower Garden*. Miss Jekyll also gave a picture of it in her *Flower Decoration* of 1907. I had long grown it in my garden without a name, calling it old cottage pink, but on reading anew the Jekyll and Robinson descriptions it all fell into place. The old leaves, lower on the stems, turn at flowering time to dark crimson, and this helps in identifying it. So my old cottage pink and 'Emperor of China' are one and the same thing. And a very old established true perennial without foibles it is, needing no annual propagation from cuttings or division. It reaches about four feet, and, usually first opening in early November for me, is an admirable cut flower just when other sources of them are getting scarce. It seems to thrive in any fertile soil. Since discovering its right name I have given it to many people. It is now listed by over two dozen nurseries.

One of the very last perennials to show its flowers is *Chrysanthemum nipponicum*. The photograph was obtained one day in early November. It thrives at the University Botanic Garden at Oxford in a sunny border of limy, gravelly soil and grows remarkably well. As a general rule, most Japanese plants seem to prefer acid soil. The dark leaves and pure

Chrysanthemum nipponicum

white, short rayed daisies are very welcome so late in the year, accompanying as they do chrysanthemums and colour forms of *Schizostylis*. The plant takes kindly to division in spring.

The cimicifugas are statuesque stalwart perennials of great quality, thriving best in soils which do not become dry. As a general rule they appreciate some shade and make themselves the more valuable by flowering towards the autumn when many plants are past their best. All are ornamental because of their large divided leaves, which are yellow in autumn. They are commonly called bugbane, from the ancient use of *Cimicifuga foetida* as an insect repellant; the generic name alludes to this use. *C. foetida*, from north-eastern Asia, is noted for tall, arching growth, and leaves and sepals of soft yellow enclosing the stamens. The topmost spike of the branching scape arches over considerably, making it unique among bugbanes so far as I know. Its flowers have a scent reminiscent of a brandy bottle, or the water lily, *Nuphar*. All species I believe have strongly fragrant leaves, which certainly has its uses in bug-ridden places.

For many years I have grown a plant called *Cimicifuga ramosa*, a name with apparently no foundation. It is accordingly with much pleasure I find it in *The RHS Plant Finder*

Cimicifuga foetida

Cimicifuga racemosa

referred to as *C. simplex* 'Prichard's Giant', honouring the once famous firm of Maurice Prichard, of Christchurch, Hampshire, whence so many good plants came. There is no doubt it is a giant of a plant: even in my comparatively dry soil it has achieved some seven feet. But let me say a little about these elegant plants. Like *Actaea*, which we have already looked at, and *Thalictrum*, which we shall see in a later page, their main attraction is from the stamens, not the petals, and their prettily divided leaves. And it is a far cry from plants in other genera of the Ranunculaceae to which they belong—*Eranthis*, *Delphinium* and *Aconitum*.

'Prichard's Giant' has the most elegant foliage of them all and sends its creamy white spires aloft, well above it. The roots are deep questing and almost woody. Since its introduction in 1879 from districts between Russia and Japan *Cimicifuga simplex* has in the course of many years' cultivation given us excellent cultivars in addition to 'Prichard's Giant', including 'White Pearl' and a group with coppery purple leaves that show off the flowers especially well. Nobody knows the origin of the excellent 'Elstead Variety', a plant launched by that wizard among nurserymen, Ernest Ladhams, some time in the 1930s. Apart from its obvious charm of foliage and wands of flowers, the buds are enclosed in mauve petals. The best known of all bugbanes, I suppose, is *Cimicifuga racemosa*, from eastern North America whence it reached us in 1732. It is always a superb sight in July at the Royal Horticultural Society's garden at Wisley, and, like *C. simplex*, has variants with brownish or purplish leaves.

It may seem strange to include a clematis here since they are mostly woody climbers. But *Clematis hirsutissima scottiae* is a herbaceous plant that dies down to a woody base in winter. It throws up branches well clothed in rather glaucous leaves above which are nodding flowers well poised on erect stalks. They bear little resemblance to any of the usual clematis flowers, being neither large nor opening flat. In fact they are bell-shaped, and do not open. The sepals are pinched together at the apex. Among plants within the species there is wide variation in colour, but one seen at Treasure's Nursery, in Herefordshire, had flowers of soft grey-lilac, paler within and hairy. They are not showy but intriguing, and are carried for several weeks in summer. The plant, a native of the Rocky Mountains of North America in cultivation since the end of the last century, used to be known as *C. douglasii scottiae* but is now called *C. hirsutissima*. Even so, it is not a plant to take the world by storm, but has charm and is different from all other clematises except those of the Viornae group. It thrives in any fertile soil except perhaps chalky ones.

Most of us have grown or seen at sometime those delightsome little weeds *Corydalis lutea* and *C. ochroleuca*. The former has yellow flowers and pale green leaves; the latter, creamy white with somewhat glaucus leaves, is much rarer. In both the leaves are daintily cut, and they are obviously closely related but I have never seen what could be taken for a hybrid between them. They seed themselves abundantly and prefer the cooler positions in any soil. *C. nobilis*, a very different plant, is a native of Siberia and was known as long ago as 1783. For all that it has never been a common plant though quite amenable to cultivation in reasonably cool positions in our gardens. The foliage is only slightly less lacy than that of *C. lutea* and the pale yellow flowers, each accentuated by a small dark blotch on the lip, are borne in substantial heads at the tops of leafy stems. It makes a deeply questing root.

Clematis hirsutissima scottiae

Crepis incana

From south-eastern Europe comes *Crepis incana*, a tufted perennial for well drained soils in full sun. In my experience it flowers well only in spells of dry sunny weather and at such times can be seen thriving in the garden at Crathes Castle, Kincardineshire, in eastern Scotland. There is something particularly winsome about its daisy-flowers held above the divided leaves. It can be raised from seed or root cuttings and is best planted, or disturbed, only in the spring.

It is a far cry from the saxifrages of our rock gardens and alpine houses *to Darmera peltata*, which has also been known as *Saxifraga peltata* and *Peltiphyllum peltatum*. It is a bog plant that, at the side of a stream will cover the soil with its iris-like rhizomes and bind it against floods. I think it was A. T. Johnson who wrote about fishing in a stream, standing safely on a projecting platform of its massive roots. The surprise is that in early spring the dead-looking rhizomes send up great stems covered in reddish hairs, to a height of two or more feet, bursting at the top into a rounded head of pink stars. By the Royal Horticultural Society's lake at Wisley, in Surrey, these appear even before the garden has been tidied up. Later, when spring has merged into summer, similar hairy stems hold large, rounded, coarse leaves joined to the stems at their centres. They last in beauty until autumn, often taking on warm tints before succumbing to frost. *D. peltata* was brought from California in 1873 and has proved quite hardy in Britain.

One of the plants that comes instantly to mind whenever the herbaceous border is mentioned is the *Delphinium*. But just as there are all kinds of herbaceous (or mixed) borders, so are there many kinds, and some surprises, among the delphiniums. To start with it does not do to think of them as entirely of shades of blue. Among the species all three primary colours—red, blue and yellow—are to be found, which is a rare gathering. Nobody can deny the magnificence of well grown hybrid delphiniums in blue, purple, white and cream, ascending to some seven feet, but there is also a red-flowered species, *D. nudicaule*, brought from California in 1869. It has been a hesitant denizen in our gardens ever since—short-lived, but easy to raise from seed. It seldom reaches more than a foot in height and seems easy to please in regard to soil and situation. The same cannot be said for a second species, *D. wellbyi*. It has been in cultivation, fitfully, for nearly as long as *D. nudicaule* but is not entirely hardy. Why then do I include it here? For two reasons: one is that I hope this book will reach the hands of gardeners in warmer climates than mine; another is that it is *sweetly scented*. Now it seems to me that such marvels have been achieved by breeding red cultivars from *D. nudicaule* that an attempt is due to infuse into these noble plants some of the fragrance of *D. wellbyi*. Would not this be a wonderful achievement? It is a native of Abyssinia and was named in 1898.

I have a special corner of my heart for old clove carnations. They are a neglected breed. In my acid soil they are not with me for long and cuttings have to be struck every

Darmera peltata (*Peltiphyllum peltatum*)

Delphinium nudicaule

Delphinium wellbyi

year. But on limy, rubbly soils, in full sun they may make woody bases and thrive for years. Their beautiful glaucous foliage is a joy through the summer months but it is not until all the summer flowering pinks are over that they start to flower. During July and August my father liked to have a dark red clove carnation in his buttonhole; the soil in his garden at Cambridge—heavy and limy—suited them. But what exactly is the Old Crimson Clove? I wish I knew. I have been given many, supposedly the true thing, but according to records (and Oscar Moreton's *Old Carnations and Pinks*) the petals should not be serrated. If so I have never seen it. At Atcham, near Shrewsbury, I have seen how successfully these old cloves will grow when suited. And the *scent* has to be sniffed to be believed. Three rich crimson old cloves have been found in Irish gardens by Nigel Marshall, head gardener at Mount Stewart; all are sumptuous and beautiful, and a reminder to us of the riches waiting to be discovered in old gardens.

The Old Salmon Clove is another of these treasures. It has been known also, erroneously, as 'Raby Castle', which is a great house in County Durham. Apart from the fact that these old cloves do well in that county and elsewhere in the north of England, I cannot suggest any reason for this adopted name. Its real name, of undoubted authenticity, is 'Earl of Chatham', named in about 1750. The Earl of Chatham was the elder William Pitt, the famous Prime Minister, who died in 1778. The colour of the flower may be likened to uncooked salmon, and not what is known as "salmon pink" (cooked). In the right soil it is a strong grower, with distinctly blue-green broad foliage. Nigel Marshall found a sport from it, depicted in *Perennial Garden Plants*, in which the petals are striped with white. It is as vigorous and fragrant as its parent, and has been named 'Phyllis Marshall'. I have found several other striped kinds, all without names.

It all goes to prove that these old jewels are being neglected. We need a national collection so that their merits can be compared and their nomenclature sorted. Mr

Dianthus 'Old Clove' with *Tagetes*

Dicentra chrysantha (left and above)

Moreton gave careful descriptions of several in his book. Unfortunately, unlike the old pinks, they apparently have no champion today. An August fossicking might reveal much bounty.

First introduced in 1836, *Diascia rigescens*, from South Africa, faded away in this country until found again by B. L. Burtt around 1980 in the Eastern Cape. It was the first of several diascias I came across making a wonderful show in the Northern Horticultural Society's garden at Harrogate, in Yorkshire. It has not proved a reliable perennial with me and, like the others, has a peculiar soft tone of pink in its flowers—somewhere between coral and rosy lilac. In warmer climates it would no doubt be a great success, but I shall have to make do with *D. fetcaniensis*, which is hardier, being deciduous, but has not the magnificence of *D. rigescens*. All the species have been taken much to heart recently by the gardening world and I think it will not be long before a hardy hybrid arrives with all the good points of the genus, including the rarified colours. They do not seem particular about soil, thrive in what sunshine we in Britain can offer and, except for *D. rigescens*, which can be a little taller, rarely exceed a foot in height. Propagation by cuttings or seeds is easy.

On a warm day in summer Brian Halliwell, at Kew, took me to see his pride and joy of the moment, *Dicentra chrysantha*, growing splendidly in poor gravelly soil and enjoying bright sun and the extra heat reflected from an old brick wall. Most dicentras that I know have light green foliage and prefer a position on the cool side, but *D. chrysantha* comes

Diascia rigescens

Dictamnus albus

Dictamnus albus and *D. albus purpureus*

from California and obviously (from its silvery foliage and its performance at Kew) appreciates all the sun we can give it. It was such a surprise too, to find it had yellow flowers, all others in my ken being of some tone of pink. I suspect it may not be long lived, except in ideal conditions, and from its stance I presume it has a tap-root. Whatever its fads and peculiarities, it is well worth all the care we can give it. It was first known in our gardens in 1852 but I think there have been long intervals when it was absent.

We cannot ascribe to *Dictamnus* any date of introduction, this native of southern Europe having been cultivated since Roman times. It is a long-lived plant, easily established in any friable, fertile soil in sunny positions. The roots delve deeply and it should be planted when quite young and not disturbed when large. *D. albus* is looked upon as the species; mauve flowered plants as its cultivars. All have stalwart stems and plenty of divided leaves, bearing at the apex of the stems in early summer airy spires of intriguing flowers, white in *D. albus*, dusky mauve-pink in 'Purpureus'. When raising them from seed, with the prospect of three or four years' wait for flowers, it is valuable to know that plants with white flowers have leaves of paler green than those with dark ones. Lovely though the flowers are they are not the end of the story, for handsome seed-pods of purplish brown mature during late summer and are quite ornamental. Moreover, to justify the plant's name of Burning Bush, these pods give off a volatile oil. On still, hot days a lighted match held beneath them will suddenly develop a puff of flame without harming the plant. Its old garden name is Dittany and, as might be expected from the oily smell of the plant, it belongs to the Rue Family.

Poor Professor Zauschner of Prague, who had the genus *Zauschneria* named after

Epilobium canum (Zauschneria californica cana)

him all those years ago; his plants we are now urged to regard as epilobiums. His memory suffers the more as *Epilobium* includes so many bad weeds. Even so, plants we once called zauschnerias are slightly woody perennials from California and neighbouring states, and have the distinction of being pollinated by humming birds. All are at home in well drained soils in hot sunny positions. Perhaps the best of them, *Epilobium canum*, brought over to Europe early in this century, has narrow silvery leaves that contrast delightfully for weeks on end with the tubular scarlet flowers. The show continues from late summer until autumn closes in. It will slowly and happily colonise a hot dry bank, and the flowers are well shown in such places. But it may be found invasive where summer moisture is generous. Propagation is easy from cuttings in early summer.

I suppose if I had to single out one Sea Holly for special attention in a garden it would be *Eryngium alpinum*. The leaves are quite handsome but the flower heads, lasting many weeks in beauty, are superb. Each knob of minute blue flowers is surrounded by a wide, much-fringed calyx, like a doily. They are borne on strong, self-reliant stems over the handsome tuft of foliage. It thrives in sunny positions in any well drained soil and should be left alone when established. Its roots are strong thongs and may be cut up into short lengths for use as cuttings or it can be raised from seeds. The flower heads, picked when at their best and hung up to dry, make long-lasting ornaments. In the garden I find it an admirable contrast for phloxes, but I have not been so successful in growing *E. proteiflorum*. To start with it is not so hardy and long lived but there is no gainsaying that it is a beauty. The flower heads, as the photograph (taken at Nymans, Sussex) shows, are of glistening, gleaming, steely white. It comes from Mexico, and in common with most South American eryngiums its leaves are narrow, long and spiny. It is best raised from seeds, which may sometimes be found in lists under the name of 'Delaroux'—the botanical authority for the name of the species.

Eryngium alpinum

Eryngium proteiflorum

Euphorbia characias var. *sibthorpii*

Euphorbias are very much the "in" plants of today. (Their enthusiasts sometimes reveal their obsession, calling them "euphorias".) They are of two kinds: European euphorbias, most of which are semi-shrubby with stems that last two years before flowering; Asiatic species, which are truly herbaceous. In the first group among hardy kinds, *Euphorbia characias* is the biggest, producing strong stems up to about four feet from a woody base, well clothed in narrow leaves and giving rather the appearance of a gigantic bottle-brush. Through the summer, autumn, and winter these are waving masses of soft greyish green; by the end of January they start to form buds and to nod, erupting in spring into ever-growing dense cylindrical heads of typical greeny yellow. They last through till June when they turn into yellowing seed heads and may be cut away. *E. characias* is a native of the western Mediterranean countries and has green flowers with brown eyes. Much more desirable from a garden point of view is its subspecies *E. characias wulfenii* whose flowers, bracts and stalks are usually of bright yellowish colour and wider in the head. Many specially good forms have been propagated (from basal cuttings taken when small with a heel) such as 'Lambrook Gold', selected by Margery Fish, and 'John Tomlinson'. They presumably originated from the botanical form *sibthorpii*.

The above represents the greatest size that any species of general hardiness will grow; one of the smallest, *Euphorbia myrsinites*, is also from southern Europe. Its trailing stems well set with glaucous leaves make an admirable picture when sprawling over paving. The flowers go through the same ritual often ending up tinted with pink in July. It was included in Gerrard's *Herball* of 1596.

The same date may be given for our knowledge of *Euphorbia palustris*. Although this epithet indicates "of the marsh" I find it is perfectly at home in any normal garden soil,

Euphorbia schillingii

Euphorbia palustris

Euphorbia myrsinites

Euphorbia wallichii

Filipendula palmata 'Rubra'

as, indeed, are all the rest. It is not only beautiful in flower but is a waving mass of lovely greenery until autumn changes its tint to yellow.

Of equal beauty, though taller and bigger, is *Euphorbia schillingii*, which Tony Schilling brought from Nepal in 1977. And then there is the rare *E. wallichii* of the 19th century introduction from the Himalaya. This is a real gem whose leaves, with white midribs, show off so well the flower heads of greenish yellow which last in beauty for months. It flourishes in the Royal Botanic Garden, Edinburgh.

I have found them all, and such others as I have grown, quite happy in any fertile soil, well drained, and preferably in sun. The species mentioned do not take kindly to division and are best increased by basal cuttings or by seeds. Especially on hot days, when pores in the skin are open, the white juice from leaves or stems can burn and irritate.

Originally all filipendulas were called *Spiraea*, but that has been changed, so that our next plant is now recognised as *Filipendula purpurea* 'Elegans'. It has not had an easy time of it, for it used to be called *F. palmata* and *Spiraea palmata*, a name applied at one time or another to eight different plants. All very confusing. *F. purpurea* 'Elegans' is an easy plant to grow, so long as the soil is moist, and has flower heads of pleasing clear pink over handsome, divided leaves. The woody rootstock presents no difficulty in transplanting in autumn or early spring. It came to our gardens in 1823, from Kamchatka, and is undoubtedly quite hardy.

From its pointed spiky seed pods resembling cranes' bills are derived the *Geranium's* common name. Other genera in Geraniaceae link up with similar derivations, thus *Erodium* is from *erodios*, Greek for heron, leading to Heron's Bill, and *Pelargonium* is from *pelargos*, for stork, giving Stork's Bill. They may have ample seed-holding capacity but it is a wary gardener who can capture the pods before they explode on ripening. Our most conspicuous native is *Geranium pratense*, the Meadow Cranesbill, to be found in grassy places

Geranium pratense 'Plenum Violaceum'

on roadside verges and the like from south to north of the British Isles, overtopping the herbage with its sheaves of blue-violet flowers in summer. It has deep-questing roots and thrives in a variety of soils so long as they are not boggy. It has long been cultivated for its beauty of leaf and flower in our gardens. Since it is so rampant of increase by its seeds, sterile double forms are more favoured as garden plants; they are easily increased by division. While the species is known, as I say, in bluish tones, white, and diaphanous pale mauve in a plant sometimes called 'Silver Queen', the doubles are available in the normal blue ('Plenum Caeruleum'), white ('Plenum Album') and the vastly superior 'Plenum Violaceum'. The first two, while undoubtedly doubles, are somewhat inconclusive and ragged in their doubling, whereas 'Plenum Violaceum' has the perfection of shape only equalled by a rose. Each petal is cupped and they create together a perfect rosette. The warm violaceous colouring completes the picture. All the coloured forms are, like foxgloves, richer in the cooler north.

In addition to the beauty of its flowers *Geranium pratense* excels in beauty of leaf. The basal leaves, long stalked, are deeply and elegantly cut and make a handsome podium for the flowers. Of soft green, they fortunately last in good shape until the autumn, when some of them colour well. The best late foliage is supplied by plants whose old flowering stems have been removed.

The somewhat awkward name *Geranium* × *riversleaianum* commemorates the once

Geranium × *riversleaianum* 'Mavis Simpson'

famous Riverslea Nurseries in south Hampshire owned by Maurice Prichard & Sons. (It was here that the hybrid *G.* 'Russell Prichard' occurred in the early years of this century.) The parents of *G.* × *riversleaianum* are considered to be *G. endressii* and *G. traversii*; the former hails from the Pyrenees and is a completely hardy good garden plant and ideal ground-cover, whereas the latter is a native of New Zealand and is not reliably hardy in the British Isles. Be this as it may, the hybrid does not suffer. Nor does it increase much at the root, but annually throws out long stems that not only make excellent ground-cover but flower for many weeks, even unto frost. The flowers are of soft chalky pink held over a mass of small leaves of a greyish tone—a perfect colour scheme. It is *G. traversii* which provides the silvery foliage in another similar hybrid, 'Mavis Simpson', which cropped up on the Kew rock garden in 1980. Somewhat taller, its flowers are of cooler pink, toning well with the silvery foliage, and like those of 'Russell Prichard', are produced from midsummer until frosts stop it. With *G. wallichianum* and its forms and hybrids, including 'Syabru', no other low plants in my experience have such a long and satisfying flowering period. I should give them all sheltered sunny places in good soil and I shall be surprised if they do not come up to expectations. They can be increased by careful division or basal cuttings in spring.

Few hardy plants have a more distinguished appearance than *Glaucidium palmatum*. We might expect this from the fact that it is grouped botanically with peonies, themselves

Geranium × *riversleaianum* 'Russell Prichard'

Glaucidium palmatum

of aristocratic bearing. But true to its lineage it will not put up with cavalier treatment in the garden and for its success demands cool woodland conditions in a retentive soil well supplied with humus. Then if suited it will produce for you, from a short rhizome, those huge, angled leaves of fresh green and the diaphanous flowers, huge in proportion, with four large petals of cool lavender and creamy stamens. Few plants have more quality. There is a white-flowered form of equal beauty, called *leucanthum*. It will set seed in ideal conditions and these are a ready though slow means of increase; it may also be divided in early autumn. This beauty is a native of Japan.

Long years ago, when I was a student at the University Botanic Garden at Cambridge, Mr E. A. Bowles, that famous gardener, brought as a gift a yellowish hellebore labelled *Helleborus kochii*. I have had my stock of the plant from this source for all these years and it has never set seeds. This is partly perhaps because it flowers in January, with *H. niger* and the garden plant we call *H. atrorubens*, whereas from its appearance, we might expect it to flower along with all the *H. orientalis* forms, in early spring. Because it does not seem to agree with the descriptions of *H. kochii* I have always distributed it as 'Bowles' Yellow'.

It thrives in heavy, limy soils in part shade, such as at Polesden Lacey in Surrey, but not in my acid sandy soils in which all the *orientalis* forms and hybrids do so well. I put all this on record because sixty years ago there were practically no Lenten Roses, as they are called, in tones of primrose yellow other than this. Of late years that indefatigable worker Helen Ballard produced many yellows, using *H. cyclophyllus*, and very good they are; but they do not flower so early as my 'Bowles' Yellow'. It is depicted in my book *Colour in the Winter Garden*. It increases reasonably freely from divisions to be made just as it is going out of flower.

The other hellebore that I have brought to these pages, *H. lividus*, is from Majorca. This is best grown in sheltered conditions in the United Kingdom, or even better in a coolhouse or cold frame, for it is not wholly hardy. Apart from the beautiful veined and marbled leaves it has rosy green flowers in a handsome posy at the top of the stem for, like the hardy *H. argutifolius* (*H. lividus corsicus*), from Corsica, it belongs to the group with woody stems, which produce their flowers in their second year. Moreover the flowers have a sweet scent which will permeate the air of a cool house on a sunny day. This delicious odour is often passed on to hybrids between the two, known as *H. × sternii*. On the very first day that I attended the meetings of RHS Committee B, I took flowers of this hybrid, crossed by myself, but it was turned down. However the next year Sir Frederick Stern showed similar flowers and secured the Award of Merit. Both *H. lividus* and its variety *corsicus* are easy to grow in almost any well drained soil in sun or shade and set plenty of

Helleborus lividus

Hieracium lanatum   *Hylomecon japonicum*

seeds. Further hybrids have been made with *H. niger*. Gardeners' first sight of *H. lividus* was in 1710 but no doubt it has come and gone over the years.

One of the very oldest plants in our gardens is the Sweet Rocket or Dame's Violet, *Hesperis matronalis*. It hails from southern Europe and Siberia and was first mentioned in 1350. This was the single-flowered species, a plant easy to grow from seed in any friable soil in sun. It is deliciously scented, in which it resembles the garden Stock, but its leaves are dark green, unlike those of the Stock, which are soft grey green. It is a comparatively short-lived plant but is easy to raise from seeds. The same cannot be said of the rare double varieties in white or pale mauve. They have been in cultivation a long time and, though of short life, are easily raised from basal or stem cuttings, and well worth the trouble. I think they all thrive best in a limy loam in full sun and are worth studying—and smelling.

We should not look at most hieraciums in our gardens except to pull them up, for they can be weedy nuisances. But *Hieracium lanatum*, which used to be known as *H. wald-steinii*, from southern Europe, is an exception. In any well drained friable soil in sun it will make the most beautiful broad leaves, covered in white or silvery grey woolly hairs. These alone would make the plant worth growing but its flowers are bright yellow daisies of no mean attraction borne from white woolly buds and stems.

Just the opposite may be recommended for my next plant, the Japanese woodlander and diminutive treasure *Hylomecon japonicum*. It belongs to the Poppy Family and thrives in cool conditions, on ledges of peat or in the rock garden. It increases fairly freely and may be divided after flowering. It has no fragrance, but when once seen is not likely to be forgotten, its fresh, neat leafage overtopped by the cool yellow poppy-flowers at about eight inches. It is full of charm and beauty for its short spring season.

When one thinks of the flamboyant flowers of *Campsis* (*Bignonia* or *Tecoma*), the Trumpet Vine, it is not a very far cry to transfer them to pink-flowered herbaceous plants: *Incarvillea delavayi* and *I. mairei*. These are most substantial plants in leaf and flower and present us with semi-hardy plants of the Bignoniaceae. Few plants can compete with their handsome lobed leaves and great trumpet-flowers in warm colourings. Commemorating one of the most famous French missionary-botanists, the Abbé Delavay, who lived in western China for many years, *I. delavayi* is a handsome upstanding plant of some two feet. The dark green leaves contrast well with the reddish stalk holding a head of several great blooms in summer, rose-red. They all spring from a fleshy tuber which, for safety, should be planted deeply. In my experience the tubers gradually weaken and die away, but in more fertile soil the opposite should be the norm. Plants of both *I. delavayi* and the shorter *I. mairei* flourish at Keillour Castle, in Scotland, proving that cold weather is not their enemy. This second species, which used to be known as *I. grandiflora brevipes*, is as handsome as the former one but less than half the height and with even larger flowers. They are often available from bulb merchants and should be planted in early spring. 'Bees Pink', 'Frank Ludlow' and 'Nyoto Sama' are separations of note. Plant them deeply in rich soil in sunny positions and hope for the best. The seeds are attached to a placenta in each pod, which is not without beauty of its own.

Incarvillea delavayi

Incarvillea mairei

Both species make extremely good companions to *Iris kerneriana* whose light yellow flowers make for the perfect contrast in colour. They were first grown in our gardens at the turn of the century, 1900.

Incarvillea olgae, a native of Turkestan, named in 1880, belongs to a group of species with leanings towards shrubbiness, or at least with a shrubby basal stem supporting a dainty mass of finely divided, dark green leaves. Over these in summer are held pink tubular flowers on wiry branching stems. *I. olgae* seems to grow best in gravelly soil in full sun and in these conditions it can be seen in excellent health in the Hillier Arboretum, Hampshire. It does not increase fast but could no doubt be divided in spring. I have not detected fragrance of any note in any of the species.

I find it difficult to understand why *Inula oculis-christi* is not better known. It is a most attractive daisy in light orange, neat of growth and free-flowering. I saw it at Herterton House, near Wallington, Northumberland, the nursery of Mr Frank Lawley and the one of so many choice plants. Though I was most kindly given a plant it did not thrive for many years; perhaps it did not find dry Surrey to its liking and pined for the cool air of the north. It obviously belongs to the Compositae or Daisy Family and like its sister species is noted for the extremely narrow rays, though there are plenty of them to make a substantial flower head. The leaves are not particularly notable and it can be increased by seed or division in spring. In my estimation it is one of summer's most attractive flowers and should be more often grown, considering that it first flowered in the United Kingdom in 1759, having been brought from eastern Europe.

My next is a small plant, but where would our gardens be without the toys? *Jeffersonia*

Inula oculis-christi

Jeffersonia dubia

dubia (sometimes labelled *Plagiorhegma dubia*) is a surprise, for it is a member of the Berberis Family, as its yellow sap would indicate. But there the resemblance seems to end. It is a lowly plant seldom achieving more than eight inches when in flower. The leaves are inclined to be two-lobed (but not so noticeably as in the larger species, *J. diphylla*) and opening on their delicate stalks are tinted soft lilac or violet—a perfect complement to the little six-petalled flowers of pale, cool lavender-blue. It is difficult to think of a more perfect combination of tints. The seeds, in pods that also betray the *Berberis* relation, are one method of increase, but plants can also be divided, preferably in earliest spring. It is a charmer of stalwart growth so long as it is given a cool position. Its home is in Manchurian woods and it was first seen in our gardens in the early years of this century.

Kirengeshoma palmata is another surprise, for it is classed with the hydrangeas. It bears no obvious resemblance to them but is a self-reliant perennial for cool, moist positions. The stems rise to four feet in really good conditions, displaying their opposite, broad, lobed leaves—something like those of a Plane Tree—to advantage. At the end of the summer, until autumn, its ebony stems are a-dangle with thick-petalled, pale yellow shuttlecock-like flowers. In the normal species from Japan they nod and sway delightfully, but in the form reputedly from Korea the stems are firmer and the flowers are borne aloft. This form is perhaps a more satisfactory garden plant but to my eyes lacks the undoubted delicate charm of the original Japanese introduction of 1891. The plant from Japan is depicted in pencil in my *Perennial Garden Plants*.

Another small plant for our pages is *Lathyrus vernus*, which was first grown in 1629. For all that, and the fact that it is a sound perennial, it is not often seen today. It belongs to the Pea Family and makes a hardy rootstock from which arise numerous small leafy shoots bearing clusters of rich purple vetch flowers. A variant has flowers of pink-and-

Kirengeshoma palmata

Ligularia dentata 'Othello'

Ligularia 'Gregynog Gold'

Ligularia macrophylla

white and there is also a pure white; all are captivating in late spring and early summer and are soundly perennial. They are, again, garden toys of the best quality; these variants are mostly shorter than the normal purple species, which in the deep somewhat limy soil at Hidcote, Gloucestershire, may achieve a foot or more.

For many years a plant in gardens has been known erroneously as *Centaurea* 'Pulchra Major'. I find it should be called *Leuzea centaurioides*. (*Centaurea pulchra* is an annual from Kashmir.) Our plant is a good perennial in any drained soil and enjoys sunshine. The leaves are deeply cut, upstanding, and grey beneath; the stems bear large Knapweed flowers of pink in brown, papery bracts. It lasts a long while in flower and grows best from spring division or root-cuttings.

There comes a time, past midsummer, when many yellow and orange daisy flowers come into bloom. They are not quite what one wants as companions to the phloxes, being at the other side of the spectrum, and the welter of *Anthemis*, *Helenium*, *Heliopsis* and the like can be overpowering. But in moist gardens, though still in the sun, there is another group of plants of orange-yellow headed by *Ligularia* species from the Far East. They used to be called *Senecio* and *S. clivorum* was one of the best known. It is now *Ligularia dentata* and a very fine plant it is, associating with yellow flowered plants and those with coppery purple leaves. *L. dentata*, from China in 1900, has given rise appropriately to forms whose leaves are dark blood-red underneath, toning with their dark stalks. 'Othello' (1915) and 'Desdemona' (1940) seem to me to be identical and reproduce fairly closely from seeds. 'Moorblüt' is perhaps richer in colour. They all make imposing clumps of large rounded leaves topped by branching stems carrying numerous wide-rayed daisies of refulgent orange. They are easy from division but, I repeat, must have rich moist soil.

Of somewhat mixed parentage is a magnificent hybrid called 'Gregynog Gold', raised about 1950 in a famous Welsh garden. Its exact parentage is unknown but it is thought to be *Ligularia dentata* crossed perhaps with *L. veitchiana* and possibly *L. wilsonii*; it is sometimes attributed to *L. × hessei*. Its flowers are an equally good colour but are borne in a handsome tapering spike. It is quite spectacular when seen with dark red-purple phloxes.

My third is a much rarer plant, brought from the Orient in 1896 but for some reason never really taken to heart by the gardening public. It is *Ligularia macrophylla*, otherwise known as *Senecio ledebourii*. Its foliage is indeed "*macrophylla*" and its flower spikes as notable as any.

When we think of the little *Lobelia erinus*, so popular in summer bedding displays, baskets and window boxes, it comes as something of a shock to realise that there are giant lobelias in Africa and that in our gardens may be found perennial plants up to four feet which make a striking display in crimson and other colours. But so it is: *L. cardinalis*, *L. fulgens* are both red, while *L. syphilitica* is a good blue. From them have been bred numerous bright garden plants of every colour in between. The blue-flowered species is a more tolerant garden perennial than the reds, in fact *L. cardinalis* and its progeny are only to be considered as perennials in soil that remains wet in winter. The most famous hybrid, of ancient lineage, is 'Queen Victoria', which combines spikes of lipped flowers of brilliant crimson with coppery purple leaves. The two tints together give a wonderful display for weeks in August, and at Lyme Park, Cheshire, in the windy formal Dutch-style garden, they are given support by canes dyed to match the foliage.

The admixture of blue in the colouring of *L. syphilitica* has resulted in a widely different series of tints in the varied progeny verging towards cerise and purple. The hybrid 'Eulalia Berridge', raised at Annesgrove, in Ireland, nearly fifty years ago, shows this veering towards the blue tones. I often think how fortunate it was that Miss Berridge was christened "Eulalia", which is of course, the name of a genus of beautiful grasses. There are several dozen named clones of these hybrid lobelias; they are invaluable for adding richness to our summer borders, especially damp ones.

I would like to put in a plea for greater use in our gardens of the perennial Honesty, *Lunaria rediviva*. Here is a self-reliant plant of some three feet which has the wit to flower just as the daffodils are going over and continuing for several weeks. The passing of the daffodils—"Fair daffodils we weep to see you haste away so soon"—is always a period of sadness for me; the first glory of a perennial has gone for another year. The biennial Honesty helps to fill the gap. While I should always choose the white ('Alba') or the rich purple-crimson form ('Munstead Variety') which we owe to Miss Jekyll, I have a soft spot

Lobelia 'Eulalia Berridge'

Lychnis × *arkwrightii*

for the cool lilac-white of *L. rediviva*. It is a true perennial with a handsome pile of good leaves, and will sow itself when suited. But if you pick the pods and dry them, as likely as not the results will be nil. The ordinary Honesty has nearly orbicular pods, which are like silver pennies and much used for drying; they earn for the plant its name of Moonwort. The pods of *L. rediviva* are elliptical and might earn for it the name of "Halfmoon Plant". It has been cultivated in our gardens since the 16th century and is well established on the outskirts of the water garden at Cliveden, Buckinghamshire.

It would not be right to call the *Lychnis* we know as *L.* × *arkwrightii* a good garden plant, because it is inclined to be short-lived and is beloved by garden molluscs, but it gives such a bright spot of colour that I am prepared to forgive it. It is of mixed parentage: from an early cross between *L. fulgens* and *L. coronaria* some not very good plants accrued which were called *L.* × *haageana*. Crossed again with the vivid vermilion *L. chalcedonica*, *L.* × *arkwrightii* materialised. This all happened early in this century and the hybrid is still around, which goes to prove that if your scheme warrants the inclusion of its colour (a little less domineering than that of *L. chalcedonica*) then here it is, and well displayed in the water garden at Longstock, Hampshire.

It is difficult to believe that such a prodigious flowerer as *Malvastrum lateritium* has really been in cultivation since it was brought from South America in 1840. Though not

Malvastrum lateritium

altogether hardy with us, it sets abundant seeds that germinate well. It is a sprawling somewhat woody member of the Mallow Family and should be given a hot sunny corner against a wall. There, the more sunshine it gets, the more flowers it will produce, and what flowers they are. I know nothing more intriguingly beautiful—small cups of soft tangerine-orange with darker, even reddish, centres. And they are borne all along the trailing branches well set with dark green, lobed leaves. It is not particular about soil and scorns drought. In a corner of my garden where it seldom gets any rain it dies down after cold winters, to come up again as soon as the weather warms up in summer.

Blue poppies have always had an allure for us gardeners. It all seemed so unlikely in the 1920s before Kingdon Ward's introduction of *Meconopsis betonicifolia* (then known as *M. baileyi*) burst into bloom. But there it was, an amenable perennial if you could give it the soil and conditions it needed. Its requirements, as for all species of *Meconopsis*, are a cool atmosphere and lime-free soil well mixed with humus. Many of us who live in southeastern England cannot hope to achieve these prerequisites without artificial means. Mecca for us is the Royal Botanic Garden at Edinburgh. Some other northern gardens and those in parts of Wales and Ireland also display blue poppies well.

A notable date connected with blue poppies is 1937. In that year a Mr Sheldon crossed *Meconopsis betonicifolia* with *M. grandis* and I think there is no doubt that the hybrid named *M.* × *sheldonii* is the most successful and brilliant of these poppies, in particular the plant which through a strange sequence of events has become known as 'Slieve Donard', after the erstwhile famous nursery in Northern Ireland. The full story is in my *Perennial Garden Plants. M. betonicifolia* has one topmost flower on a stalk of a few inches and other

Meconopsis quintuplinervia

Meconopsis × *sheldonii* 'Slieve Donard'

flowers lower down the stems of some four feet, in leaf axils. The basal leaves are many and Betony shaped. *M. grandis* on the other hand has equally good leafage and stem, but the flowers are borne on long stalks separating from a central point. The plant called 'Slieve Donard' is intermediate and can be considered a true perennial in the right conditions, easy from division in early autumn or very early spring. The colour of the flowers is true spectrum blue and needs to be seen to be believed. It has just that brilliance that most other blues lack.

By a fortunate chance long years ago at Cambridge I became acquainted with a doctor from Leeds, who sent me a plant of *Meconopsis quintuplinervia*, the Harebell Poppy, which I had read about in the limpid prose of *The English Rock Garden*, by Reginald Farrer. By giving it peat purchased from the local seed shop at about one shilling and sixpence per peck I was able to keep this exquisite plant for a few years. It is a sound perennial when suited in cool surroundings and throws up from the mass of hairy leaves below, tall stems each a-dangle with one lovely light lavender blue bell, darkening towards the central cream stamens. As with others of its tribe, the Harebell Poppy is well seen in northern parts, especially at the botanic garden in Edinburgh, where they all do so well.

Meconopsis punicea, first introduced in 1909, became lost and was only brought to Britain again a few years ago. It needs, in fact demands, all the coolth obtainable and I was

Meconopsis × *cookei*

Meconopsis villosa

lucky to see it doing well at Kew. It is of the same habit as *M. quintuplinervia* but the wide flowers are of rich dark red. Not having grown it myself I cannot say much about its cultivation but it appears to be easy from seed and can be divided. *M. punicea* hails from western China as does Farrer's Harebell Poppy. *M. × cookei*, the hybrid between the two, was raised by Mr R. B. Cooke in Northumberland some years ago and is still grown by devotees of the genus.

Meconopsis is noteworthy in that all three primary colours—red, blue and yellow—are found among the various species of the genus. It is a specialty shared by *Delphinium*, *Aquilegia*, *Gentiana* and a few other hardy genera. There are two noteworthy yellow perennials among them, the dainty *M. chelidoniifolia*, a pencil drawing of which occurs in my *Perennial Garden Plants*, and *M. villosa*, which used to be called *Cathcartia villosa*. The former is one of the most dainty perennials I know: branching stems ascend to some three to four feet bearing hairy, lobed leaves and nodding, small, salver-shaped lemon-yellow blooms in profusion. It is essential to grow it in woodland conditions where drying winds will not shrink the leaves. The other species is much larger and coarser in leaf and flower, but no less wondrously beautiful when hanging its great lemon-yellow bells out to the admirer. While *M. chelidoniifolia* is from western China, whence it was brought in 1904, *M. villosa* is from Nepal and Bhutan and was collected in 1891. Though reasonably manageable in the right conditions they are not often seen in the south of Britain.

Nepeta govaniana

The next two plants were brought over in this century from Kashmir and both have approved of our climate and are successful garden plants. *Nepeta govaniana*, at one time known as a *Dracocephalum*, is a real charmer, a freely branching plant bearing multitudes of small, lemon-yellow, lipped flowers. While there is no doubt that it prefers some shelter from drying winds it is thoroughly at home on the sunny beds at Kew. Easy from seed, it can also be divided, preferably in spring and like the next species is not particular in regard to soil so long as it is well drained. I challenge anyone not to fall in love with the mass of pale yellow flowers, which appear for weeks in summer. I was won over by the sight of *Nepeta nervosa* on the Edinburgh rock garden some years ago. Like the former plant it has become well known and has a long flowering period, putting up spike after spike of flowers through the summer months. This also can be raised from seeds or increased by division in spring. They both have the added attraction of fragrant foliage.

Owing to their long-lived roots and their splendid flowers, peonies have been favourites of mankind since the dawn of history, and were freely depicted in early herbals, particularly *Paeonia officinalis* in Europe and other species in China. They all thrive in rich soil where their tuberous, thick roots can quest deeply. Along with other plants with tuberous and bulbous roots they appreciate the nourishment given by bonemeal and potash and when once established and thriving they should be left undisturbed. This does not mean that divisions cannot be removed, but that they should be made with as little disturbance to the parent clump as possible. Seeds, which species freely set as a rule, often take a long time to germinate and do not always appear in their first year after sowing. It is manifest that many peonies have been raised from seeds in the past, judging by the numerous hybrids that are known and grown, many of them of great beauty. French nurserymen showed the way, but wholesale raising of the popular strain was carried on in the early years of this century by Messrs Kelway, of Somerset; the efforts have now passed mainly to Messrs Klehm, of Illinois, while more unusual crosses have been made also in the United States by Dr. A. P. Saunders, of New York, and others. This is a sketchy outline and takes no account of the shrubby peonies, usually known as Tree Peonies. Although they are usually easily settled in the garden the level at which the fat root-buds (the "crowns") are set is important: nothing causes so much delay in establishing new plants as being planted too deep or too shallow. The crowns should be almost level with the soil surface.

Nepeta nervosa

Paeonia veitchii var. *woodwardii*

Every year the first peony to flower in my garden is 'Early Bird', a well and truly named triple hybrid by Dr. Saunders, dating from 1939. From a hybrid between *Paeonia emodi* and *P. veitchii* a further cross was made with *P. tenuifolia* which has narrow, even thread-like dissections of the foliage, inherited by 'Early Bird'. To this charm is added the same species' rich crimson colouring. It is a wonderful sight with *Narcissus poeticus recurvus*. The next early is one of its parents: *P. veitchii*, also with narrowed leaflets and nodding flowers of magenta. Its variety *P. veitchii woodwardii* is of a good pink, and it is worth raising a batch from seeds to pick out the ones that appeal most. Following quickly on is the suitably named 'Avant Garde', also photographed in my garden, a hybrid of *P. wittmanniana* raised by Messrs Lemoine of Nancy, France, in the early years of this century. It inherits a creamy salmon tint from that species and has spectacular coppery young foliage as a contrast.

Most of the species crowd on; one of my favourites is *Paeonia arietina*, whose greyish foliage tones well with the crimson-purple flowers, though I prefer in my garden the delicate pink of its form 'Mother of Pearl'. By some botanists it is classed as a subspecies of *P. mascula*; it has been known from south Europe and Asia Minor since 1824. These are all rather rarified species and forms, but we enter more closely into the popular garden peonies when we consider *P. peregrina*. This is a most brilliant plant with bright, rich green leaves and flowers of refulgent scarlet. It has been known as *P. lobata* and one of its garden forms is called 'Fire King', very suitably. Known since the early 17th century it hails from the Balkans.

Paeonia arietina

Paeonia peregrina

Paeonia 'Avant Garde'

My last of these handsome plants is the very old *Paeonia lactiflora* 'The Bride'—sometimes ascribed to *P. albiflora* 'Whitleyi Major' dating from the end of the 18th century, and a pure and glorious flower of, I believe, ancient Chinese lineage. A pearl beyond price. It is more fragrant than the others and has very large nearly single blooms with a pronounced boss of yellow stamens. The foliage is dark and impressive.

The flowers of single and double peonies have a short life but a glorious one. Thereafter we can enjoy the noble foliage until early autumn when not a few regale us with rich burnished tints and intriguing seed-pods that open to reveal seeds of several tints; the red ones are usually infertile, but the others should be sown as soon as ripe.

There is a little group of miniature poppies of great charm and long flowering period from Europe, North Africa and Asia Minor; they are *Papaver atlanticum, P. lateritium, P. pilosum* and *P. rupifragum.* They are all good perennials in well-drained soils and present no difficulty in cultivation. In spite of having been grown for about a hundred years they

Paeonia lactiflora 'The Bride'

Papaver lateritium

Parahebe perfoliata

are little known. I would single out *P. lateritium* because it has a particularly bland tangerine-orange tint. If the seed heads are picked off after flowering it will go on producing buds for many weeks from early summer until autumn begins. The same may be said of the others. It is I suppose the removal of the seed pods that constitute just another gardening chore that prevents their wider use today.

For long known as *Veronica perfoliata*, brought from Australia in 1834, this delightful plant is now called *Parahebe perfoliata*. In any sunny spot in good soil it will make a sprawling mass of stems clothed in rounded perfoliate leaves of smooth grey-green, so like many a *Eucalyptus* from the same continent. At flowering time in summer every shoot ends in a spike of blue speedwell-flowers which intrigue everybody. Since it is almost evergreen in favoured places, it is a garden plant of considerable value. It is easily raised from cuttings—or seeds if you can get them.

In the sunny garden at Sutton Place, Guildford, in Surrey, *Phlomis samia* var. *maroccana* thrives in sandy soil and flowers in late summer. It is semi shrubby; each procumbent stem ending in a shapely spire of palest lilac-rose flowers. The basal leaves are broad and handsome. It was collected in Morocco by Maurice Mason in 1983 and has proved reasonably hardy through several winters but is easily propagated by seeds or cuttings. This is a plant of unusual appearance for soft colour schemes in warm gardens.

In an often overlooked corner of the garden at Sissinghurst I once noticed a pleasing assortment of plants that included a bold mass of subdued pink flowers from *Phuopsis stylosa* (formerly *Crucianella stylosa*) lit by mahogany-red pansies and contrasted by the cool greeny-yellow flowers of *Alchemilla mollis*. The first of these has been known and, in spite of its rather offensive smell, grown since 1836. It is from the Caucasus, is an easy plant for any sunny spot in fertile soil, and can be divided in spring. As for the *Alchemilla*, it has been known in our gardens only since about 1948 but has become a firm favourite. This is strange because it was recorded in 1874 from the Caucasus and Asia Minor. What a plant

Phlomis samia var. *maroccana*

Phuopsis stylosa

for Miss Jekyll, had she known it! It is an arrant spreader by seed and it is best to remove the fading flowers to guard against its taking over the entire border, or garden. It is easy to divide in autumn or spring.

The Cape Figwort has long been known in our gardens—since 1855 to be exact. It is a splendid plant, *Phygelius capensis*, semi-woody but surprisingly hardy for a South African. It is well displayed on a fairly sunny wall at Hidcote, Gloucestershire, although it can just as well be grown in the open border. It should be pruned hard down in either case when during the summer and autumn each strong shoot will bear a positive plume of little tubular scarlet flowers with yellow throats. A third name, *P. capensis coccinea*, is of doubtful authenticity; I have only seen one red kind, but the 'coccinea' part is supposed to relate to forms with red throats. Also from the Cape is *P. aequalis*, which I have seen in fine form at Keillour Castle, in Scotland, the home of so many good plants owing to its very varied terrain. The two plants are much alike but the colour of the flowers of this second species is quite different; it is a soft coral-red with a lemon yellow throat and small mahogany lip. The plumes of flowers are of the same size and the dark foliage much the same. Neither species can tolerate drought. Mr B. L. Burtt, of Edinburgh, found among other coloured variants in the wild in 1977 one which he has called 'Yellow Trumpet'. This is a pleasing soft creamy yellow. They all have long flowering periods and are not particular in regard to soil.

Persicaria (Polygonum) alpinum is a highly desirable plant, not spreading unduly at the root and creating a refreshing display in early summer. It grows well at Mottisfont in the

Phygelius capensis

Phygelius 'Yellow Trumpet'

Persicaria (Polygonum) alpinum

gravelly, dry soil and puts up a good show every year. It is surprising it is not seen more often in gardens, particularly as it hails from the Alps and has been known since 1816. It presents no difficulty in cultivation and is a pleasing contrast to heavyweights like peonies and irises.

I cannot pretend that *Polygonum amphibium* is a good garden plant and in any case I expect it should now be called *Persicaria amphibia*. It is a British native, a water-weed of great vigour known as Willow Grass. I was working during the day at Wallington, Northumberland, and ventured into the countryside of an evening, coming across a great spread of its pink flowers on a lake, I think in Harwood Forest. It caught my eye and if it were not so rampageous a spreader it would be wonderful in some of our great gardens, flowering from summer until early autumn.

I should not like to be without the autumn-flowering *Persicaria (Polygonum) vacciniifolium*. It is a prostrate plant that makes good ground cover and fine curtains on walls. This is a key to its success: I find it susceptible to cold, drying winds in winter and spring, many shoots drying, but there are usually two or three pieces left which root at the nodes and throw up plenty of little pink spikes in early autumn. Its tenderness is probably due to cold coupled with dryness for it is a native of the Himalaya. It is a winsome little carpeter for the end of the season and first saw light in our gardens in 1845.

Persicaria virginiana used to be called *Tovara virginiana*. The green-leafed normal type has given way in gardens to two attractive variegated forms which last in beauty through summer into autumn. Of two plants in the Royal Horticultural Society's garden at Wisley, Surrey, the older has attractive leaves marked, striped and spotted with cream.

Persicaria amphibia

Persicaria vacciniifolium

Another variant, 'Painter's Palette', has red-brown markings as well, splashed with pink. I have not observed flowers on either, but those of the species are of little account being airy wisps of tiny reddish dots. 'Painter's Palette' occurred in 1975 but the original variegated form has long been grown. They wake up rather late and are not at their best until late summer and autumn—and all the more valuable for it. The species comes from eastern states of North America, as its name suggests.

The Pasque Flower, *Pulsatilla vulgaris*, is a lovely plant to grow in the spring garden, no less than on its preferred site, a chalk hill. It is easy to raise, so long as you first pick off the long hairy awns from the seeds, so there is no need to go and denude its native hills, where it is becoming scarce. It prefers a stony, sharply drained, limy soil, where it will flourish for years in full sun, even seeding itself. Throughout Europe there are forms with darker, but smaller flowers, and seedsmen's strains have become mixed. All are beautiful and you may even raise a pink or a white form as well as the usual purplish shades. It reaches to only about ten inches, well be-furred with hairy and divided leaves; the stems and flowers are hairy too. But these notes are really concerned with the taller yellow *P. alpina apiifolia* which used to be known as *Anemone sulfurea*. It will reach two feet when well suited in acid soil with lots of humus. It is a native of European mountains, and has long been known.

A variegated form of *Persicaria virginiana*

Pulsatilla alpina apiifolia

Primula 'Devon Cream'

When Lionel Fortescue went to live at what has since become famous as The Garden House, in Devon, in the early 1940s he found a hybrid *Primula* growing there, like a gigantic Oxlip. I asked for a root and have always been enthralled by it, and have given divisions away from time to time. Mr Fortescue had no name for it but suggested it should be called 'Devon Cream'. I am glad to say that Beth Chatto has worked up a stock and has it available. It is obviously a hybrid, probably of the common Primrose but whence comes the clustered head of drooping creamy yellow flowers? The Oxlip (*Primula elatior*) and the Cowslip (*Primula veris*) are not natives of that part of Devon, so that one is forced to consider a polyanthus as a parent. But, strangely, it has no scent. Even in my rather light soil and dry sunny district it manages to survive but is a poor shadow of what it can be in cooler, moister conditions. In my garden it sulks for a year if divided after flowering; I think this operation is best carried out in earliest spring before the leaves have grown up. In my estimation it is a thoroughly worthy garden plant.

One of the many plants that Gerrard mentioned in his *Herball* of 1596 was *Ranunculus aconitifolius* 'Flore Pleno'. I am never sure whether this delectable plant should be called "Fair Maids of France" or "of Kent". It might be thought that such a charmer needs no champion, but strangely it did not appeal to Reginald Farrer, who preferred the single-flowered species. This, in moist ground will make a mass of white buttercups over handsome, dark, fingered foliage a yard high and wide. The double form is not so vigorous though often achieving two feet, and I for one am always captivated by the neat, very double, white button-flowers. While the single species can be raised from seeds, the double has to be divided and given a good soak; this is best done in earliest spring or immediately after flowering.

Ranunculus aconitifolius 'Flore Pleno'

As it is a native of the Azores and neighbouring countries we cannot pretend that *Ranunculus cortusoides* is generally hardy. However, seeing the plant flowering in moist ground at Mount Stewart, Northern Ireland, made me realise that in the mild though cool climate there, it had found a congenial home. It has been known and grown since 1826. The handsome lobed leaves give rise to a tall stem on which are poised splendid large buttercup flowers in spring. It can readily be raised from seed.

Ranunculus constantinopolitanus 'Plenus' has long been known in gardens as *R. speciosus plenus* and also sometimes as *R. gouanii*, which name belongs to a different plant. The Constantinople species is a handsome plant indeed, not only above ground but also below, where its woody, hairy, rhizomatous roots gather strength every year to produce a good lot of rather coarse buttercup leaves and a lavish display of fully double flowers, bright yellow with a green tinge on them from the innermost segments. In all the plant may rise to a foot high in moist soil and will form a goodly clump. It is comparatively slow of increase and perhaps this is why it is so seldom seen. Division after flowering seems adequate for its increase. I have never seen plants of the single-flowered species.

We are all used to seeing the culinary Rhubarb putting up the odd spike of multitudes of creamy white flowers, but you would have to go to what is known as a "physick" garden or botanic garden to see what a handsome plant *Rheum officinale* is. It can well hold its own in floral beauty with any other garden plant. it has long been grown in Tibet for medicine and was first known over here in 1871, but has not made a name for itself in our gardens. Probably this is because of its medicinal properties, but may also be due to the

Ranunculus constantinopolitanus 'Plenus'

Rheum officinale

fact that, though beautiful until early summer its overweening leaves then start to flop and decay making a large gap in a border. It is easily grown in any fertile soil and can be divided in late summer, autumn or earliest spring. It can no doubt be raised from seeds but that would be a lengthy process.

All the rodgersias are imposing plants for good, deep, damp soils, in sun or part shade. They are somewhat confusing and similar to each other but are helped by some of their names, such as *Rodgersia aesculifolia* (Horse Chestnut leaves); *R. sambucifolia* with pinnate leaves like those of an Elder (*Sambucus*), and *R. pinnata* itself. There are several others, and all are upstanding plants bearing their branched plumes of tiny creamy flowers well above the leaves. The podium of leaves may reach three feet in rich moist soils and the flower stems two feet or more higher. *R. pinnata* is seldom seen but its variety, or form, 'Superba', has been taken by gardeners to their hearts, and not surprisingly so for its flowers are a good rich pink. I have not been able to find its origin; all plants I have seen came originally from Rowallane in Northern Ireland. Perhaps Mr Hugh Armitage Moore raised it himself as he did so many good plants. The species has been known since 1902, when it was brought from China. While all appeal very strongly to me—adding

Rodgersia sambucifolia

Rodgersia pinnata 'Superba'

Romneya 'White Cloud'

firm lines to any assembly of plants—*R. sambucifolia* takes some beating, though its flowers are cream. At Hidcote, Gloucestershire, it thrives mightily in a moist patch of ground. After flowering the seed heads are invaluable for drying. Division of the roots is safe in the dormant season, but the task calls for a sharp spade.

The romneyas have long been garden favourites for sunny warm sites. Coming as they do from California they need all the sun they can get in our much cooler climate, where they usually die to the ground every winter. In warmer climates they make woody stems and are classed as shrubs. *Romneya coulteri*, known here as the California Tree Poppy, but as Matilija Poppy in its native California, was first seen in British gardens around 1875. When established its questing roots are not easily deterred, even by house foundations, so that one might expect it would be easy to transplant, but this is not so. While it can be raised from imported seeds, root-cuttings are the most usual means of increase. Here again it is not simple; I have found that the creeping small roots near the surface of the soil respond most readily to attempts at propagation. Some growers use roots of pencil thickness. Plants do not take kindly to transplanting when rooted afresh so that it is usually best to start each piece of root in a separate small pot and to transfer them to larger pots as they grow. While *R. coulteri* was the first known to us, another species is available—the closely allied *R. trichocalyx*, distinguished by its hairy buds. Both have the most beautiful poppy flowers with large white petals like crumpled silk and a large boss of rich yellow stamens. The foliage is glaucous. The most handsome form I have seen is at the Hillier Arboretum; said to be a cross between the two species, it is named 'White Cloud', and has larger, lovelier flowers and particularly bold grey leafage. It is best to plant them, from pots and with least possible disturbance, in spring in any fertile, drained soil in full sun.

Known from countries around the eastern Mediterranean since the 16th century, *Salvia argentea* is only fit for dry sunny gardens and is most at home when planted in a retaining wall. This is because its greatest beauty is in its thick white-woolly leaves; they are large (many inches across) and make an extremely attractive rosette. In its second or third year (it is best raised from seeds) up comes a stout stem, branching and bearing an array of white, hooded nettle-flowers in the usual style of Labiatae. Thereafter it may settle

Salvia argentea

Scabiosa (Lomelosia) minoana

Saxifraga manschuriensis

down, if well suited in regard to drainage and sunshine, to another display in the following year, but as likely as not it will set abundant seeds (in hot summers) and is best raised afresh.

It may seem strange to include two saxifrages here, since these pages are not really concerned with rock plants, but the two I have selected are plants of great character and merely demand the good drainage of beds and borders preferably nestling along a rock edge or retaining wall. I came across *Saxifraga manschuriensis* in the Bressingham nursery, where Alan Bloom and family grow so many good plants, and it took my eye as a most unusual member of the genus. I suppose it belongs to the Porophila Section and its specially handsome fleshy rounded leaves seem to demand a cool exposure. The flowers, appearing in summer, are good too. My other plant is famous: it is *Saxifraga longifolia* 'Tumbling Waters' a form or hybrid dating back to the 1930s or earlier, having been raised by none other than Captain B. H. B. Symons-Jeune who, in *The Natural Rock Garden* (1932), first showed us gardeners the correct use of rocks in rock gardens from a biological and geological point of view. I was inspired to take his ideas further in my own, *The Rock Garden and its Plants* (1989). But to return to the saxifrage, the whole point about 'Tumbling Waters' is the fact that, unlike *S. longifolia* itself, it does not die after flowering, but produces side rosettes. These can be detached and rooted to start life on their own. But the glory of the plant is those superb arching plumes of small blossoms. I think that, unlike many of the rosetted saxifrages, both *S. longifolia* and its 'Tumbling Waters' variant need a cool exposure, otherwise they tend to produce small plumes only. They also need a bit of help in the form of a gentle fertiliser to give of their best in June.

Having been given a rooted cutting of *Scabiosa minoana* by Brian Halliwell when he was Assistant Curator of the rock garden and herbaceous plants at Kew, I have been delighted to find the plant—a native of hot limestone escarpments in Crete—quite hardy and amenable to cultivation in a small suburban garden, where it gets sun only after midday. It has made a woody trunk rather in the manner of a sage and presents a dome of shoots each terminating in a rosette of spoon-shaped leaves of a few inches, silvery grey from a dense covering of hairs. Above all this for many weeks come unbranched stems each bearing a typical scabious daisy-flower of cool pale lilac-pink—a lovely soft combination. It comes easily from seed or heeled cuttings. It was introduced by Alan Burman from Crete in 1969, and Brian tells me that its revised name is *Lomelosia minoana*, but that does not lessen its undoubted beauty.

Known at one time as *Oreochome candollei*, my next plant has a distinguished past, but seems now to have fallen into disfavour. It is now known as *Selinum wallichianum* (*S. tenuifolium*). One reads of its being noted as an imposing lawn specimen in William Robinson's *The English Flower Garden*. (I wonder how much manure was spread for it to ascend to the heights of dignity shown in his illustration.) In my garden it is all it can do to reach three

Selinum wallichianum

feet. Even so it has considerable beauty with its daintily cut, lacy leaves and flat heads of snow-white tiny flowers, the whole thing like a glorified Cow Parsley. It has travelled a long way, from the Himalaya to wit, and has been known in our gardens for the best part of a hundred years. It is easily raised from seeds, in fact this is the only suitable means of increase, for it makes deep-questing tap-roots. It seems quite at home in any fertile soil, and like the Cow Parsley, is a member of the Umbelliferae.

The ordinary Comfrey (*Symphytum officinale*) is a native of Britain and Europe and has established itself in the United States as an alien. It is a beautiful plant when in flower, set with little bells of cream. Its leaves, fried or boiled, are considered a delicacy in Bavaria. It has given us a good hybrid with *Symphytum asperum*, which has blue flowers. The result, *S. × uplandicum*, yields big, rather coarse plants, with flowers in a variety of colours. But we are solely concerned here with the very fine variegated form, S. × *uplandicum* 'Variegatum', whose big leaves are of greyish green broadly edged with cream. It comes through the soil early in spring and in June may be four feet tall, bearing bunches of lilac flowers turning to blue. Thereafter it begins to look a bit tired and it is best to cut it all down, when it will make a fresh crop of beautiful leaves that stay until autumn, outlasting even the hostas. It can be increased only by careful division of the crowns, preferably in early spring. Root cuttings, so useful for the hybrid itself, are no good, for they only produce green leaves. It thrives in any fertile soil.

Thalictrum diffusiflorum is a comparatively recent introduction from Tibet. Not

Symphytum × uplandicum 'Variegatum'

Thalictrum diffusiflorum

grown in our gardens until 1938, it at once established itself as one of the most beautiful species. I have had no success with it in dry Surrey, and believe it prefers the cool moist atmosphere of the north; not only cool atmosphere but also a cool soil with humus. Certainly it was flourishing in such conditions when I saw it in Edinburgh. It makes a wiry plant of some three feet prettily decorated with small rounded leaves, and later in June with exquisite, nodding, lilac bell-flowers containing cream stamens. There are few plants of such dainty perfection so easily raised from seeds.

We looked at *Baptisia* earlier in these pages; *Thermopsis montana* bears a considerable resemblance to it except that it has an invasive root. Nobody could complain, however, about the leaves—dark green and elegantly three-lobed—topped by the spikes of lupin-flowers of clear yellow in June. It grows well at Hidcote in rough, rubbly soil and will seemingly grow anywhere except in a bog. It was brought to our gardens from western North America in 1818 and can be raised from seeds, or by division of its travelling roots.

Popularly known as the Scotch Flame Flower, *Tropaeolum speciosum* was brought from Chile in 1847. It ascends by means of its clasping leaves and will completely envelop shrubs. I have seen wired walls ten feet high covered with its scarlet flowers. It is not

Thermopsis montana

Urospermum dalechampii

Ursinea sericea

usually a success in the drier parts of Britain but is annually a great sight at Hidcote, Gloucestershire, where it clings to the north side of clipped dark green yews. In Scotland and Ireland it is a brilliant spectacle. The flowers are delightful, being fashioned like a small version of the annual plant so well known as *Nasturtium*. When the flowers are over blue berries mature. Its roots, when suited in cool moist soil, are long, thick, creamy grey threads and can be a nuisance where it thrives—but such a beautiful nuisance.

Quite a woolly bear of a plant is *Urospermum dalechampii*. We have grown it without difficulty in our gardens since the 18th century; it is a native of southern Europe and quite hardy. Its only enemy is likely to be winter wet, but nobody wanting to grow so hairy a plant would give it other than good drainage and full sun. The whole plant—leaves and stems—is dark green with a somewhat greyish sheen from the hairs, against which the bright, lemon-yellow, almost double daisies show to advantage. It achieves about one foot in height and width and is in flower for many weeks in summer. I have seen it growing and flowering well as far north as Aberdeen, Scotland; it seems happy in any well drained soil in full sun. Does not this all sound like a plant that should be grown more often?

My last Dicot is little known and deserves publicity. Coming as it does from Cape Province, South Africa, it is of doubtful hardiness and will probably not stand more than a degree or two of frost. Even so *Ursinea sericea* grew well at Mount Stewart, Northern Ireland. I doubt whether any flower-lover would not be charmed by its silver, finely dissected leaves, especially when decorated with fine deep yellow daisies in summer. It makes a compact somewhat shrubby plant a foot or so high and wide and flowers for a long season. It should be given a sunny warm site in sharply drained soil such as would be found on a rock garden. *U. sericea* could not for long put up with the damp climate at Mount Stewart and eventually succumbed after a few years of joy and beauty.

Cortaderia selloana

PART THREE

Hardy Grasses

The snows are fled away, leaves on their shaws
And grasses in the mead renew their birth,
The river to the river-bed withdraws,
And altered is the fashion of the earth.

More Poems, v, Diffugere Nives
(Horace: Odes IV, 7), A. E. Housman

In the Temperate Zones of the world I suppose a greater area of its land surface is covered by grasses than by any other section of the flora. It behoves us therefore to give them due consideration.

There is one very important cultural detail to be established in regard to grasses, a section of the Monocots. Never divide nor transplant the wholly deciduous species in the autumn; they will probably die. Defer all work with them—including cutting down the old leaves—until the spring has really arrived, with warm weather. In Surrey I leave cutting down, dividing or transplanting until May, often late in the month. If some green shoots are showing, all well and good; if not delay still further. Of the grasses mentioned in this book that injunction does not concern the *Milium*, but it applies to many species of *Carex*. It is no use thinking that a spell of warm sunshine in March is a good time; do not be tempted; I have lost hundreds of cortaderias in my nursery garden days through too early lifting and division.

Fond as I am of the majestic *Arundo donax* from south Europe, I think it is a bit large for the average garden. It is a spreader, too. But its variegated form, whose broad grey ribbon-like leaves are striped fully with creamy white, is a special favourite. Alas, it is less hardy than the type. In Beth Chatto's garden, near Colchester, Essex, a clump of the variegated *A. donax* is planted out only for summer effect along with cannas and other tender plants. Like the species, it can be divided, and can also be increased by cuttings made from sections of the stems or the occasional side shoots.

Arundo donax 'Variegata'

Chionochloa conspicua

Chionochloa conspicua, a native of New Zealand, has been known as *Cortaderia* or *Arundo conspicua* and at one time was called *Danthonia conspicua*. Just how confusing are the grasses mentioned in these pages will be discovered as we go on. At Mount Stewart a position sheltered by evergreens was chosen for *C. conspicua*, and it had the benefit of afternoon sunshine. I am not sure how hardy it is, for the climate in that part of Ireland is gentle. Its creamy-silvery panicles of flowers are compelling in late summer, and the foliage is reasonably compact. It would be a wonderful contrast to phloxes and the tall lobelias.

I am surprised that *Cortaderia fulvida* is not more grown. It is the first alphabetically of the genus, which contains *C. selloana*, the well known Pampas Grass. But first let us look at the New Zealand species, *C. fulvida*. It has the inestimable merit of flowering in early summer, is always graceful, with nodding, one-sided plumes of flowers, which on opening are soft fawn-pink. It is a rare plant. Mrs J. B. Muir found it and grew it well at Kiftsgate Court, Gloucestershire, where it is, fortunately, still to be seen. Apart from one other instance in Gloucestershire and at Chelsea Physic Garden, London, I have seen it nowhere else. I had it at one time, but it died in a cold winter. It can be raised from seed from New Zealand and is a plant of great beauty. It is the first of all the Pampas Grass relatives to flower; just at the crown of the summer when roses and many other treasures are at their best.

If you travel through Scotland and the north of England in autumn you will see a tall grass, manifestly a Pampas relative, waving its graceful, wispy, arching plumes up to six feet or more, oblivious to cold and wet. It is *Cortaderia richardii*, the New Zealand Toe-toe grass. It is hardier than the real Pampas Grass, which is not seen much in the north of these islands. Sometimes it is called *C. conspicua* in error.

Cortaderia fulvida

Cortaderia richardii

Cortaderia selloana 'Monstrosa'

Cortaderia selloana 'Rendatleri'

When we come to the true Pampas Grass, *Cortaderia selloana*, from South America, we find a plant that has been taken to heart by gardeners ever since it first flowered in Ireland in 1842. It is so much a favourite, displaying its silvery, creamy plumes in the October sunshine, that one occasionally sees it planted as a specimen in tiny front gardens. It is a plant suitable to the grandest surroundings and is admirably planted and displayed in Sheffield Park Garden, Sussex, where it makes a superb contrast against dark conifers and the brilliant autumn colours of the trees and shrubs specially planted for this effect.

There are several named forms of *Cortaderia selloana* to be sought. That known as 'Sunningdale Silver' has magnificent, wide, feathery silvery plumes, borne strictly aloft in a bunch. 'Monstrosa' on the other hand has equally large or even larger plumes but they have a wide grace and are suitable for the best of great plantings. 'Rendatleri', known since 1873, is quite different in colour, being light lilac-pink, and tall and upright. The col-

Cortaderia selloana 'Pumila'

Milium effusum 'Aureum'

ouring comes from unopened stamens within the flowers; they lose much of their lovely tint in maturity. The one disadvantage with all these great plants is their wide-spreading mound of leaves. The wind moves them around and when planted in lawns hanging tips rub and kill the grass. On the other hand a form called 'Pumila' has much shorter leaves without this disadvantage; its plumes are dense and erect but only about five feet high. There is no doubt that it is the best for smaller gardens. The leaves of all kinds are sharp to the touch. The best way to tidy up a clump after the winter is to set light to it on a dry day; the blaze is soon over and will not harm established plants.

A friend in California tells me that *Cortaderia jubata*, similar to *C. selloana* and also from South America, has escaped from gardens there and is now a serious pest in coastal areas where winters are mild. *C. selloana* was believed benign, but there is some evidence that plants choking out native vegetation include hybrids between *C. jubata* and *C. selloana*. Perhaps nurserymen in California should be encouraged to stock instead the prettily variegated forms coming on the market from New Zealand; these are not, so far as I have seen, so vigorous as the norm.

I have a great weakness for the yellow-leafed form of the Wood Millet Grass, *Milium effusum* 'Aureum', found by E. A. Bowles, I believe in Norfolk, many years ago. It fortunately reproduces itself from seed (sometimes too freely) with surprisingly few green reversions. It is one of the prettiest spring pictures when contrasted with blue scillas of any sort, its young foliage being bright gamboge yellow. Later it sends up two-foot stems daintily flowering in the same tint. When mature, or before, these should be removed to prevent seeding. If given a good soaking the clumps will then send up a crop of fresh good leaves.

By July the flowers of *Pennisetum orientale* will be in evidence over the short grassy leaves. The stems reach to about eighteen inches and bear long feathery heads much like some great hairy caterpillar. When first developing they are full of colour, the long awns being of rich glistening lilac; later the whole inflorescence becomes soft pale brown. I have always found it hardy but it is not without suspicion, hailing as it does from south-west China and north-west India. But I saw it growing well in a Wiltshire garden. It is perhaps the grass most susceptible to dry springs and should not be divided or planted until that season is well advanced.

Fritillaria persica 'Adiyaman'

PART FOUR

The Monocots

On every road I wandered by
Trod beside me, close and dear,
The beautiful and death-struck year:
Whether in the woodland brown
I heard the beechnuts rustle down,
And saw the purple crocus pale
Flower about the autumn dale;
Or littering far the fields of May
Lady-smocks a-bleaching lay,
And like a skylit water stood
The bluebells in the azured wood.

A Shropshire Lad, XLI, A. E. Housman

We have now reached the part of the book concerned solely with the Monocots. Their leaves are often smooth, generally much longer than wide, and have parallel veins. To me the Monocots have a generally more distinguished appearance than the Dicots, containing as they do some highly august genera such as the lilies and Day Lilies, the hostas, Lily of the Valley and others. Also included are the grasses, sedges and rushes. To these I have given a special chapter because they are a group all on their own and are pollinated by wind, which, to me is a sign of humbler origin than those needing the agency of insects or even birds.

Unlike Dicots, whose flower-parts are often in fives, the Monocots' flowers are made up of threes. This is amply demonstrated by those lovely woodland plants the trilliums, which have three leaves, three calyces, three petals, three stamens; and what, at school, we used to call the seed-box, has three compartments.

The fact that the veins of the leaves are parallel instead of netted does not result in all Monocot leaves having a narrow shape such as we see in grasses, bamboos and palms;

they may be broad and even inclined to be lobed or triangular, as in *Arum* and *Zantedeschia*. It seems to me that they all have an air of good breeding in their leaves, no less than in their flowers, which are often of surpassing beauty. I have only to cite *Lilium*, *Iris*, *Gladiolus* and *Hedychium* to prove this. Are they not in a class apart from the Dicots? And their roots are not just a mass of threads or fibres but have a shape all of their own: bulbous or corm-like; rhizomatous, as in many irises and Solomon's Seal; or merely thickened as in Lily of the Valley.

Taking them as a whole the Monocots are just as easy to grow as the Dicots and have a similar number of likes, dislikes and foibles for us to study and circumvent. Their great value in the garden is a quieting contrast of suave foliage, but they need the contrast of the leaves of the Dicots no less. It is this, coupled with size and stance, that makes the gardens of today so interesting. There is no doubt that whereas a hundred years ago the accent was on floral colour, today the value of good and varied foliage is much to the fore and creates what has come to be studied under the cognomen of "texture". To achieve this to the maximum we need *both* groups blended and interspersed for contrast and satisfaction. Two of the most disparate groups are the ferns and grasses; contrast them with hostas, bergenias and rodgersias and your garden picture is half done and of lasting beauty, to be completed with flowers, which come and go.

Today there seems to be a wholesale preoccupation with grasses in parts of Germany and the United States. To my mind they are most appreciated when greater contrast of foliage is used rather than the interplay of similar leaf-forms. An assembly of various grasses seems to me to be just as indigestible as any other grouping of one kind of plant. The contrast need not be upsetting or too diverse if the groupings of things and scale are deeply studied. This is of course the crux of the whole matter. While flowers tend to come and go at short notice the leaves are with us for months on end; therefore their study is of paramount importance in planning a garden.

Agapanthus 'Loch Hope'

Allium cristophii

Allium karataviense

Having looked through a few grasses we can now consider the Monocots in general and I am glad to find them headed alphabetically by those very good plants, the Blue African Lilies (some are white), or *Agapanthus*. Long known and grown for pots and tubs *A. africanus* is a magnificent plant with bold heads of small blue lily-flowers. It is evergreen and thus not hardy in most parts of the British Isles. Since the Second World War a great step forwards has been achieved, largely by the initial interest and energy of the Honourable Lewis Palmer, who in his chalky garden in Hampshire raised a lot of hardy forms and hybrids of *A. campanulatus*, also from South Africa. From *A. africanus* the main difference is their being deciduous and hardy, with flowers of all shades of blue and white only slightly smaller than the old species.

I find *Agapanthus* 'Alice Gloucester' a good white, and 'Cherry Holley', a good blue, pleases me especially because it produces secondary heads of flowers after the main crop. Both of these are about two feet high but 'Loch Hope', raised at the Savill Garden, Windsor, by Hope Findlay is a splendid large grower perhaps up to four feet with large heads of rich dark blue. It is colourful in the Savill in September grouped with variegated Pampas Grass and golden cypress. There is nothing quite like these African lilies; their leaves are smooth, dark green and strap-shaped and the rounded heads of small lily-flowers are long lasting. They are happy in any fertile garden soil, divide easily in spring, and their papery pods, containing black seeds, are useful for drying.

Beautiful as the heads of the various species of *Allium* (Onion) are, they are best cut away before the seeds are ripe because they are such arrant spreaders. I suffer from this neglect in my own garden, where *A. aflatunense* and *A. cristophii* have colonised large patches of ground. *A. cristophii* is one of the most handsome of all species. The soft blue-green leaves come through the soil, as do so many of them, early in the spring, but by flowering

Alstroemeria ligtu hybrid

time are, unfortunately, becoming rather tatty. But one forgives all faults when the flowers are open—great globes of amethyst stars on stout stems, glinting in the sun. It is a native of Turkestan and we had it in our gardens as long ago as 1901, growing it then under the name of *A. albopilosum*, referring to the cottony hairs covering the leaves. It was planted at Sissinghurst, Kent, with *Fuchsia magellanica* 'Thompsonii' and the white form of *Geranium sanguineum*; perhaps it still is.

The next onion, *Allium karataviense*, was splendid filling a stone-edged bed in the formal garden at Knightshayes Court, Devon, dominating with its broad leaves a planting of geraniums, including *Geranium sanguineum striatum* (*G. lancastriense*), *G. sanguineum* 'Shepherd's Warning', and in the foreground *G. argenteum* 'Alannah'. The contrast of flower and leaf-shapes makes a pleasing pattern for many weeks in early summer. *A. karataviense* is also from Turkestan having been named in 1878.

In gardens where choice plants are grown alstroemerias are not uncommon. The old orange-flowered *Alstroemeria aurantiaca* has given place to the hybrid between *A. ligtu* and *A. haemantha*, which occurred in British gardens where the two species were planted after being collected in Chile in 1925. *A. ligtu* has been known since 1838. It still grows in an unadulterated state at Kiftsgate Court, Gloucestershire, in stiff somewhat limy soil, and is pure glowing pink. The lily-like flowers are borne on large, branching heads over poor foliage. The admixture of *A. haemantha* has resulted in a lot of startling flame shades as can be seen in a large bed of them at Oxford University Botanic Garden. Lovely though they are, the pure pink of *A. ligtu* surpasses all the shot shades. They all have fleshy, tuberous roots which are not always easy to transplant and are best raised from seeds, one in each little pot to avoid root disturbance. When a year old they are ready to be planted out; their roots are sometimes susceptible to frost and if they can be planted in a depression and earthed up as they grow this damage will be lessened. They have no fragrance to speak of, but their seed capsules are ornamental when dried.

Saint Bernard's Lily, or *Anthericum liliago*, is a native of the Alps and has been known and grown since the 16th century. While it is a lovely and attractive plant in early summer, flowering with early peonies, it is less impressive than the form known as 'Major', or sometimes *A. algeriense*. Above strap-shaped grey-green leaves arise stately stems well set along their upper length with flat, star-shaped, snow-white flowers well seen at Hidcote, Gloucestershire, in limy rich soil. It has fleshy roots but is easy to divide and replant in early spring; it is constant from seeds, but they are not produced prolifically.

Looking at *Arum creticum* in full flower one would be surprised to hear that it is quite hardy, so exotic does it appear. But it has long been grown at Hidcote, Gloucestershire, on a raised bed which must have been frozen solid in many winters. The tuberous roots throw up spear-shaped dark green leaves in late winter, to be strongly contrasted and overtopped in early summer by the intriguing creamy yellow arum-flowers with their projecting yellow spadices. Then it all dies down, to produce red seeds in late summer. In spite of being quite hardy and having been brought from Crete in 1928 it is little known. It can be divided after flowering.

Although we depend for colour in our gardens mainly on shrubs in the first half of

Anthericum liliago 'Major'

Arum creticum

Asphodeline lutea

the year, when June comes the King's Spear, *Asphodeline lutea*, is not readily passed by without appraisal. It is easily grown in any reasonably drained fertile soil in sun and can be divided in autumn or early spring. The bulbous roots send up a sheaf of narrow blue-green, grassy leaves from which arise stately stems set closely with straw yellow, starry lily-flowers, silky and fragrant. The buff-coloured bracts warm the overall colour effect. Later, round green seed pods materialise, and these are not without beauty and use when dried. King's Spear has been in our gardens for hundreds of years.

There is always a floral gap in the garden just after the daffodils go over—unless you grow tulips—which is hard to combat with perennials. There are flowering shrubs in plenty for this period, but fewer herbaceous plants. One genus that helps us over the gap, and that I should like to see enjoyed more is *Camassia*. The bulbs are a delicacy when cooked by the American Indians, but with plant prices as they are today I cannot think one would buy any for the pot. Though they increase fairly readily, they are not common. They have rather untidy long leaves, and upstanding spires of starry flowers in various tints from the several species, some rather wishy-washy, others, ascribed to *Camassia leichtlinii*, of a rich blue colouring as in 'Eve Price', raised a few years ago at Wakehurst, Sussex,

Camassia leichtlinii 'Electra'

Camassia leichtlinii 'Plena'

and named by A.D. Schilling. One of the very best is 'Electra' raised about 1960 by Eric Smith. This is a big stalwart plant—again with untidy leaves—which has good-sized flowers of steely blue in tall spikes. Rather late in the season comes *C. leichtlinii* 'Plena', with creamy double rosette-flowers in tall spikes. It is a fine plant, but in early seasons the topmost flowers are apt to be browned by frost. They are all of easy cultivation in any fertile soil, can be safely divided after flowering, and do not need staking though they may reach to four feet.

With the exception of one or two Umbellifers I suppose *Cardiocrinum giganteum* must be considered the most magnificent perennial; its stems may be as much as four inches through at the base and the leaves a foot across, heart shaped, of dark shining green. Imagine these great stems giving of a series of leaves of diminishing size all the way up the stem, then ceasing and giving way to great lily-trumpets about one foot long in a spike which may top ten feet. They are wonderful to look up to and into, of greenish cream contrasted by a mahogany-red flush in the throat. The resulting seed heads are spectacular. Although I said it is a perennial it requires some knowledge and care to make it give of its best. It needs very rich moist soil in sheltered woodland conditions. It is best raised

Cardiocrinum giganteum

Cautleya 'Robusta'

from seeds (which take several years to reach flowering age) from which the most impressive spikes materialise. After flowering the bulb dies but generally leaves two or three young bulbs; these should be separated and grown in fresh rich ground. Their spikes are seldom as tall as seed-raised stock. When planting, the bulbs should be near the level of the soil.

There is no doubt that this, the Giant Lily brought from western China in 1841, is one of the most magnificent of all hardy plants. It was at one time known as *Lilium giganteum*, but the heart shaped leaves separate it from *Lilium*. It performs famously at Wakehurst, Sussex, where it flowers in early summer. In woodland gardens in New Zealand's South Island it is said to naturalise and be something of a nuisance, but who could possibly complain?

There are not many hardy plants in the Ginger Family, but the *Cautleya* known as 'Robusta' is one of the few. The leaves, beautiful, long and pointed, clasp somewhat the lower portions of the stems, which ascend to about three feet in any fertile, reasonably moist soil in sun or part shade. The fleshy roots increase readily and are suitable for division in spring. It is not until summer is beginning to wane that the flowers appear. They are dark yellow, strongly contrasted by the rich red-brown of the bracts. Later, blue berries in almost white capsules mature. Its origin does not appear to be known; it is a garden plant and not to be confused with the species *C. robusta*.

Crinum × *powellii* 'Haarlemense' is a superior form of the well known hybrid between *C. bulbispermum* and *C. moorei*. In addition to great bulbs and lanky leaves, all forms produce abundant flower-stems when established in warm positions against sunny walls. Of the normal two forms, pink and white, I find the white 'Album' superlatively beautiful,

Crinum × *powellii* 'Haarlemense'

Crocosmia 'Carmin Brillant'

Dierama pulcherrimum

the ordinary pink one not so good. But 'Haarlemense' is a superior pink form raised in Holland which should be sought. They are all on the borderline of hardiness but seem quite happy in our British gardens, including that of Talbot Manor, in the exposed eastern county of Norfolk.

At the moment of writing a lot of interest is being shown in the innumerable forms and hybrids of the hybrid *Crocosmia × crocosmiiflora*. An incredible number are being found in old gardens, brought to light and compared. And there is astonishing variation in them, which is not altogether surprising when we consider that the original cross between the nodding yellow *C. aurea* and the erect-flowered red *C. pottsii*, both from South Africa, was made in France by Messrs Lemoine in 1882. Since then further hybrids have been made, mostly in Norfolk, in the early years of this century. But they did not find much favour in gardens because it was considered they needed lifting in autumn and storing against frost. Two of the most colourful of the old hybrids are 'Carmin Brillant' and 'Vesuvius', both raised at the turn of the 19th century. Though carmine is rather a stretch of the imagination where these plants are concerned—all are on the yellow side of the red of the spectrum—there is no doubt that both stand very high in quality of plant and bloom. Though both species are from South Africa, we should not be misled into thinking of them needing hot, dry conditions. They must have ample moisture and do best in the milder, damper west of England. Of late years Alan Bloom has led the way with new hybrids with *Crocosmia masoniorum* and what we used to know as *Curtonus paniculatus*, with spectacular success. All the kinds discussed, and others, are successful from spring division and all have decorative light green narrow arching foliage, creating graceful weed-smothering clumps.

Wand Flower and Venus' Fishing Rod are the two popular names applied to this most graceful of all hardy plants, *Dierama pulcherrimum*. It has been in cultivation for many years from South Africa, and is a member of the Iris Family. From a bulbous root erect leaves, less than an inch wide, reach to about two feet. Over them waves and sways the tall arching wiry stem, or sometimes a small cluster of stems, hung with silky purple bells on exaggeratedly long thread-like pedicels. Forms have been raised with flowers from white to crimson, and from pink to wine purple and all are beautiful. Since its introduction to Britain, in 1825, chance hybrids of *D. pulcherrimum* and *D. pendulum* have occurred in gardens, and during the early years of this century the Slieve Donard Nursery, in Ireland, raised a number of hybrids with *D. dracomontanum*. These were listed in their catalogue as 'Heron', 'Kingfisher', 'Skylark', and so on, and may persist unrecognised in some gardens. Having in mind the wide natural variation of height, flower colour and size within the species, and the crossing that may have taken place with plants of other species, the diversity of plants passing for *D. pulcherrimum* is best enjoyed for its beauty, but not warranted for authenticity. But no matter the provenance, the hardiness of dieramas, though not

Erythronium 'Pagoda'

without question, may be judged from the fact that some thrive in southern and western Britain and Ireland, and in the garden at Inverewe, western Scotland. They are best planted in spring and seem to thrive in all soils other than bog or pure chalk.

It is difficult to single out just one Dog's Tooth Violet when all are so beautiful. While most of us know and grow the European species, *Erythronium dens-canis*, with its beautiful marbled leaves and daintily poised lily-flowers of lilac-pink as soon as the snow-drops are passing over, some of the American species, which follow on almost immediately are even more beautiful and taller. My special favourite this year—they are all so breathtakingly beautiful that one's estimate of their beauty varies from year to year—was a hybrid called 'Pagoda'. A suitable name too, for a flower of soft Chinese yellow poised in sprays of two or three over the handsome leaves. Each flower is a daintily recurved mandarin's hat. They have no fragrance but have every other asset associated with the Lily Family. They can safely be lifted and divided as soon as the leaves show signs of wilting but must be kept moist while out of the ground and planted as soon as possible at the right depth. They may take a year's rest after transplanting but the eventual reward is sure. They are quite hardy in my garden.

Fritillaria pallidiflora

Named and grown in 1887, from South Africa, *Eucomis pallidiflora* is still seldom seen. Perhaps this is not surprising for it has pale greenish starry flowers in a stout spike with a crown of pineapple leaves at the top, and rather large flopping leaves. At Sissinghurst, Kent, it grows in a south facing border. It might not be hardy up the country, but is dependent upon moisture as well as warmth. It should be planted in late spring in any fertile soil and can be divided when the crowns become congested and the spikes small.

While the Snake's Head Lily, *Fritillaria meleagris*, is well known in the wild and as a garden plant, some of the species from southern Europe are seldom seen. Some have a horrid habit of the corm splitting up after flowering. Flowers are no more seen—until and if, that is, the bulblets get stronger. At the University Botanic Garden at Oxford—a sunny garden on gravelly, limy loam—both *F. pallidiflora* and *F. libanotica* seem quite at home. The former has greeny-creamy bells heavily spotted with red-purple within, in all about a foot high, whereas the latter offers a species of some two feet hung with dusky purplish bells covered with a grey-white bloom. In leaves neither is remarkable. They should be planted at a depth of about six inches in early autumn. *F. pallidiflora* hails from southern Siberia; *F. libanotica* from the Middle East. This used to be called *F. persica* and

Galanthus 'S. Arnott'

the form 'Adiyaman' is generally found to be the strongest and most reliable grower. They can both be raised from seeds but it would take several years for them to flower.

The enthusiasm for snowdrops (*Galanthus*) has been growing ardently during the last half-century or so and collections of over a hundred different species and cultivars are not uncommon. Is it not a dangerous thing to single out just one of them for honourable mention? It might be thought so, but not when you have seen and grown the hybrid 'S. Arnott'. Mr Arnott was a keen and observant gardener in England in the early part of this century. He wrote frequently about his plants in the gardening magazines of the times. Although there are snowdrops today with larger flowers—witness 'Cicely Hall', 'Beth Chatto', 'Mighty Atom'—there is not one, I venture to say, that has so many good points as 'S. Arnott'. I have been growing it for about forty years in very sandy soil and also in a better loam and it has proved a good doer the whole time, increasing regularly. The leaves, though considerably broader than those of the common snowdrop, *Galanthus nivalis*, are narrow and grey-green. The stems are vigorous, reaching to nine or ten inches. They carry a large flower of generous proportions and well rounded outline, the inner segments showing a neat green mark at their apex. It is scented, so far as snowdrops go. But I think it is the generous rounded outline that makes it instantly recognisable in a collection. It seems to me to have all the qualities we desire in these flowers of the early year.

I am not pretending that *Hedychium gardnerianum* would grow in my garden. It was

Hedychium gardnerianum

brought from northern India in 1819. It grows in favoured gardens in the south west of these islands, including Trengwainton at the extreme of Cornwall, where we may see what imposing plants these are when in flower. The foliage is borne all up the five-foot stems, broad sheathing blades of rich green. *H. gardnerianum* is more usually seen in greenhouses but A. D. Schilling, of Wakehurst, brought back from Nepal a splendid, dignified form of *H. densiflorum* in 1966 and named it after his daughter 'Tara' in 1982. This is a fine species, taller than *H. gardnerianum*, but with rich orange flowers in place of the other's yellow, and it has proved to be hardy. They are not particular in regard to soil but it should be moist and in full sun. The magnificent heads of flowers are produced in late summer. The rhizomatous roots travel slowly in one direction and if, as I did, you plant them pointing in opposite directions you may end up with the stems a yard apart. They should only be disturbed in late spring and all have a delicious scent.

I approach day lilies with some diffidence. My favourites among them are old and out-of-date varieties, and I persist in my opinion that present-day hybridising and selection are ruining this noble genus of plants. Instead of breeding them with the floral segments reflexed almost into a ball, would it not be better to concentrate on the true lily-shape of the flowers? Their beauty is amply illustrated in my garden by *Hemerocallis fulva* var. *rosea*. It came from China about 1930 and has a beauty and refinement little in evidence among today's multitudinous seedlings. Further, the gracious flowers are poised well above the leaves, which are not coarsely broad. The opposite can be seen in the variety 'J. S. Gaynor' raised by George Yeld in the early years of this century: while the flowers are good the stems do not hold them clear of the leaves. As to colours, I favour the light yellows—most of which are well scented—and other pale hues; they blend more easily

Hemerocalis fulva var. *rosea* and 'J. S. Gaynor'

Hippeastrum pratense

Hemerocallis 'Kwanso Variegata'

with other plants than do the muddy mauves and hot oranges now in vogue. As to the red flowers, I have seen nothing to rival 'Missenden'.

The variegated garden plant called 'Kwanso Variegata' (Kwanso being merely Japanese for day lily) was brought from Japan in the late 19th century. This attractive variegated plant is not a form of the big, double, apricot-orange, old Japanese garden plant we call 'Kwanso Flore Pleno', introduced to us in 1860. It has inferior double flowers and is apt to revert to green, when it is called 'Green Kwanso'.

Although day lilies can be transplanted at almost any time, I favour the spring. Portions of the dense roots can be chopped off with the spade with every hope of success. Those descended from *H. fulva* and *H.* 'Kwanso' have wandering roots and are best avoided in small gardens.

Now we come to a bulbous plant that, though brought to us from Chile in 1840 and quite hardy, is little known and grown. *Hippeastrum pratense* has been growing out of doors at Blickling Hall, in cold Norfolk, for many years and annually regales us with its blazing vermilion-red trumpet flowers in early summer. The leaves are dark green, smooth, long and shiny. The bulbs should be planted several inches deep in sunny positions in any fertile soil in autumn or early spring. It is a startling flower enlivened by yellow stamens, and is also known as *Habranthus pratensis*.

Like the day lilies, hostas have been subjected to a vast amount of hybridising and selection, particularly in England and in America. Apart from 'Aphrodite', a double form of *Hosta plantaginea*, and one or two other doubles, the flowers have not suffered any "im-

Hosta fortunei 'Albopicta'

provement"; the hybridising and selection have been wholly concerned with the leaves. There is no doubt that these plants are *par excellence* the foliage plants for all gardens that have a modicum of shade, or full shade. They are easy to grow in any fertile soil other than pure chalk or a bog. Their enemies are the garden molluscs; a few however seem resistant to them. Not so the white and pale yellow variegated forms, which seem particularly attractive to them.

Visitors to Beth Chatto's garden near Colchester, Essex, will have seen a variegated hosta (*H. fortunei* 'Albopicta') contrasted by *Kniphofia* 'Little Maid' and one of the tall bright crimson lobelias and will know just how effective it can be. I gather that most nurseries find 'Frances Williams' the most popular of variegated hostas; to the broad glaucous leaves it adds a wide band of yellow.

Of the many hostas that have been raised and named during the last quarter-century I think few approach so nearly to true blue in their leaves as 'Halcyon', one of several of the Tardiana group by Eric Smith. In fresh young leaf, with the flowers of the azalea 'Naomi' in my garden in June, it is a striking sight. Later it puts up a particularly good show of the usual lilac-tinted lily-flowers, which blend so well with the leaves. It is a compact plant specially suitable to the small garden. Like all hostas it tolerates division at almost any time of the year. Garden molluscs do not seem to be fond of its leaves.

One of the most sought after is the slow growing *Hosta tokudama* 'Aureonebulosa'. This has small, somewhat cupped, leaves of good glaucous blue-green, splashed with yellow-green. When my deep interest in these plants began I was intrigued to see this first at Crathes Castle, Scotland, and also in Lady Moore's garden near Dublin. I did not come across it elsewhere.

Hosta 'Frances Williams'

Hosta 'Halcyon'

Hosta tokudama 'Aureonebulosa'

Hosta 'White Colossus'

Today there is every imaginable variegation to be found amongst the infinite number of forms that have evolved; none I think is more striking and refreshing on a hot day than Paul Aden's 'White Colossus', which I admired at Bressingham Gardens, Norfolk. But be sure to give it the benefit of plenty of shade.

Hostas are easy to divide with spade or large knife and are quick to reestablish themselves in spring or at other times.

There are certainly four, perhaps more, irises with leaves striped with creamy white or yellow. Because iris flowers are generally rather fleeting, this variegation has value in the garden. One of the most striking in spring is *Iris pseudacorus* 'Variegata', discovered so long ago in 1903. *I. pseudacorus* is the genuine Fleur de Lys of medieval days. Unfortunately the leaves of the variegated form lose their colouring at flowering time and revert to green. Although it will grow in any moist soil it is best by the waterside. *I. laevigata*, best in shallow water rather than merely beside it, also has a variegated form the cream and green striped leaves of which make such a pleasing contrast with the lavender-blue flowers in summer. There are two variegated forms of *I. pallida*: 'Argentea', with creamy white variegation from a rather poor flowering form; 'Variegata', with yellow stripes and better flowers.

The Japanese irises so long known as *Iris kaempferi* now are called forms of *I. ensata*. These thrive best in really moist soils, acid or neutral, with plenty of humus and rich food. The soil in the water garden at Leckford near Stockbridge, Hampshire, answers that description and a fine group of Japanese irises can be seen there. They reached our shores from Japan in 1839, and the many colour patterns of their flowers have been achieved, mainly in that country and the United States, by selection of plants entirely within the one species: *I. ensata*.

Next there are two irises of the Spuria section for which I have a special liking.

Iris pseudacorus 'Variegata'

Iris pallida 'Variegata'

Iris laevigata 'Variegata'

Several forms of *Iris laevigata* in the water garden at Leckford, Hampshire

Iris kerneriana

Among Spuria irises the falls, or lower segments of the flower, recurve sharply and with great effect. *I. kerneriana* is a native of Turkey and Armenia and seems equally at home in any fertile soil in our gardens, as does *I. orientalis* from Asia Minor, which we have been growing since 1790. This species has led to several good hybrids, one of the best and most floriferous being 'Ochraurea', raised by the redoubtable Michael Foster about 1890.

The Japanese irises mentioned above are best transplanted in September, while I think the Spurias are better moved in early spring.

These are, however, all unusual species and do not measure up in the estimate of many to the bearded irises that the average person thinks of when irises are mentioned. To me bearded irises have a unique shape so beautiful that I deplore the modern tendency to breed new ones with great flowers so frilled and goffered that the original shape is totally lost. Moreover, very often the rhizomes are long and make open house to annual and other weeds. Time was when rhizomes were short and matted, the stems slimmer and shorter (as in the category of Intermediate Irises today) and the flowers revealed that serene shape fashioned by placing two R capitals back to back. In modern iris breeding this has gone. The only things that mercifully are left to us are the crystalline texture and, in some iris flowers, the fragrance. My two examples of varieties long since surpassed are 'Gracchus', an iris of short stature with yellow and red-brown falls and heavy white veining raised in 1844, and the *Iris pallida* hybrid 'Mademoiselle Yvonne Pellitier' which was raised prior to 1929. Bearded irises demand well drained soil, full sun and exposure, and division (when necessary) in summer after flowering.

Iris 'Gracchus'

Iris tingitana fontanesii

Iris 'Mlle Yvonne Pellitier'

It was a blazing hot June day in the hot sunny garden deep in Sir Frederick Stern's south-facing chalkpit garden at Highdown, Sussex, that I saw *Iris tingitana fontanesii* and *Pancratium illyricum* growing together. Both plants like to have a really hot summer and sharp drainage to be successful. The iris is a native of Morocco and the variety *fontanesii* is generally reckoned to be its richest colour-variant, resplendent in deep violet-blue with striking orange blotch. It is about two feet in height when in flower, the recurving leaves of soft green rather longer. It has been known and grown since the end of the 19th century. Nestling by its side was the *Pancratium*, a native of southern Europe. It has broad leaves of soft blue-green, and the creamy white flowers have the characteristic short bowl or trumpet in the centre of the wispy outer segments. It is sweetly scented and has been known for nearly four hundred years. Both of these plants will thrive at the base of a hot sunny wall and any transplanting should be in early autumn for the *Iris* and spring for the *Pancratium*.

I feel it is not generally appreciated how hardy and good in our gardens are the smaller Red Hot Pokers, such as the plants that have in the past been called *Kniphofia nelsonii*, *K. macowanii* and *K. galpinii*. Now that further research has been done on them they are all classed as forms of *K. triangularis triangularis*. They seem to be quite hardy in Surrey and like most kniphofias are dependent not only on sunshine and good drainage but also

Kniphofia triangularis triangularis

on plenty of moisture. They are all in flaming colours, bright orange red, and they flower in autumn just when we need warming up. At two to three feet in height with narrow grassy arching leaves, they fit the smaller garden admirably and last in flower for several weeks. They wake up late in the spring, when they may be divided. They are from South Africa and no doubt the same provenance provided the inspiration for the charmer 'Little Maid', a seedling of 'Maid of Orleans' raised by that assiduous and expert gardener Beth Chatto in 1966. As a contrast to the others, a few late spikes are generally available; they are blandly ivory-cream but the main crop appears in summer and goes on for weeks. Further, the spikes are long and are lasting in flower. As with the others, the foliage is grassy and arching. When one thinks of the untidy mass of leaves around a clump of the common Red Hot Poker (*K. uvaria*) and its often bent and flopping massive spikes of flowers, one should be thankful for the neat brilliance of these shorter plants. They add a further dimension to the beauties of the Lily Family to which they belong.

Kniphofia 'Little Maid'

Lilium candidum, garden form

I have nothing but praise for all the ardent hybridists who have given their attention to the species of *Lilium*. So many superb hybrids have been raised since 1950, and fortunately the beauties inherent in the genus have not been impaired. It is as if the queen of flowers has remained unsullied in the hands of humans. There are lilies today of almost every colour and shape, from trumpets to stars, open or nearly closed, nodding or upright, some scented others not. Cultivation for almost all is dependent on perfect drainage, and the only enemies of the plants are botrytis and the lily beetle. But the oldest of all—in cultivation—is my favourite, *Lilium candidum*. The plant we all try to grow under this name is really a selected form of the species of unfathomable antiquity, depicted on ancient pottery in times long gone by. When the lower flowers, of crystalline whiteness, are open, topped by erect buds, I think no other species or hybrid can compare. At Mottisfont Abbey, Hampshire, where the soil is stony, limy and perfectly drained, it is happy. I used to grow it well in limy, rather sticky soil in Cambridgeshire, but not in acid soil of my present garden in Surrey. An old recipe for its success is bonfire ash. Another is that the only month for transplanting is August; this because soon after the stems have been removed after flowering new leaves promptly appear, before the autumn, to store up

Lilium centifolium

strength for flowering in late June and July. The scent is delicious and at times almost overpowering. Really healthy plants have good foliage; the bulbs should be planted with their noses just on a level with the ground. How I wish I could grow it again, but I have to be content with others.

Farrer waxed eloquent over *Lilium centifolium*, as well he might, having introduced it to British gardens in 1916. This is another species that thrives on limy soils, even chalk, and did well in the famous garden on chalk made by Sir Frederick Stern, at Highdown, Sussex. When suited it can reach six feet or so, bearing a dozen flowers—horizontal trumpets of creamy white, mahogany tinted without, flushed yellow within. They are strongly fragrant, with neat recurving leaves all up the stem. I have had this growing well even in my acid, sandy soil, but one disastrous spring, when they were about nine inches high the shoots were destroyed by frost and never did I see them again.

My tale of woe is alleviated by a lasting success with *Lilium martagon*, one of the

Lilium martagon

Lilium pyrenaicum var. *rubrum*

Lilium 'Shuksan'

Turk's Cap style, a richly coloured prolific form given to me by Mrs Muir, of Kiftsgate Court, Gloucestershire. The flowers are of deep coppery red-purple, as many as thirty on a tall, self-reliant stem, well above the whorls of good leaves. In some years, just before the flowers open, the buds are taken by mice. It beats me why they should creep up those stems, perhaps six feet tall, on the off-chance of finding something to eat. *L. martagon* has been grown in our gardens since the 16th century, or even before, and is a good sound perennial, best moved in early autumn.

Lilium pyrenaicum is another garden stalwart and is available in yellow or brick red. The flowers are nodding, of the Turk's Cap persuasion, and are also strongly scented. I had the red one growing near to *Philadelphus coronarius* 'Aureus' and the scent of the two blew right across the garden. They flower in June and should be replanted in early autumn. They seem quite happy in any fertile soil and increase freely though it must be admitted their flowers are rather small. As the name suggests, they hail from the mountains of Spain.

One of the Bellingham Hybrid lilies, raised in the United States, pleases me very much—it is 'Shuksan', the result of crossing *Lilium humboldtii* with *L. pardalinum*. These are very different from the above, thriving even in rather boggy, certainly moist, soil and the gracious flowers with segments strongly recurved are heavily spotted with dark red, murrey or brown. 'Shuksan' is one of the best in warm orange-yellow and thrives at Edinburgh Botanic Garden. The bulbs are almost rhizomatous, increasing sideways in line, and need planting some six inches deep. The series was raised in 1924 and 'Shuksan' has stood the test of time well.

We are not expecting many more treasures to open by the time September arrives, but one especial treat awaits us in *Lilium speciosum*, from Formosa and central China. It burst upon the gardening public in 1874 and has remained a favourite ever since. At Nymans, Sussex, a highly successful array of *L. speciosum* used to be grown. Unfortunately it is not the most dependable of lilies and the whole batch was eventually destroyed by botrytis, a fungoid disease spread by aphides. Botrytis was once controlled by constant spraying with fungicide, but even for the protection of this lovely lily the method is no longer in favour. Its recurving rose-pink (or white) flowers have a delicious aroma, and red warty spots, which give them an unusual appearance. It needs a well drained soil well mixed with lime-free humus and will grow in shady conditions, but I think all lilies appreciate sunshine. There is a trend today for bulb merchants to send lily bulbs out in spring with the consequence that they try to produce flowering stems before they are really established and well rooted.

It is unfortunate that the name of Skunk Cabbage has been applied of recent years to the two species of *Lysichiton*. It is quite wrong and really applies to another member of the Arum Family, *Symplocarpus foetidus*, which has lobed leaves and stemless hooded flowers that squat upon the ground like toads. The two lysichitons have immense paddle-shaped leaves, which act as good ground-cover through the summer. Like *Symplocarpus* they favour boggy ground. As with other arums, the flowers are small, numerous, and clustered on a

Lilium speciosum

Lysichiton americanum

Milligania densiflora

Narcissus 'Jana'

Narcissus bulbocodium citrinus

cylindrical spadix at the centre of a conspicuous spathe. In these two species the spathes are large and arise from the ground in earliest spring. That of *L. americanum* is a good yellow with a rather offensive odour—hence the confusion with the Skunk Cabbage—while that of *L. camtschatcensis* is pure white, rather more widely open and has a sweet scent. They both make long, deeply questing tap-roots and are best planted when quite small. They spread readily by seed and sometimes produce lovely hybrids of creamy yellow. *L. americanum* grows along a marshy stream at the Savill Gardens, Windsor, where it makes a fine picture accompanied by *Primula denticulata*.

I found a rare plant thriving at Edinburgh. It was *Milligania densiflora*, from Tasmania. It appears to be quite hardy, though I have not grown it, and it thrives in any well drained fertile soil in sun or part shade. I found something very appealing in its sprays of cream, tiny flowers. It is a member of the Lily Family and has grassy silky leaves radiating from a clump.

"Fair daffodils we weep to see you haste away so soon" is a line of Tennyson's that in spring strikes a true note. But hold hard! if we plant circumspectly we can have daffodils and narcissi in flower from Christmas until the middle of May. Is not this long enough even for a favourite flower? For there is no doubt it is a favourite flower with us all. Apart from their bright telling tints of yellow and white, there is the unique shape and poise, and often a delicate scent. Until 'Rijnveld's Early Sensation' came on the market my first early (after 'Cedric Morris' at Christmas) used to be 'Jana'. This was raised by Alec Gray, and in Cornwall it used to flower with him in January and hence the name. With me in Surrey it usually appears in February and lasts a long time. The large bulbs do not increase quickly but produce flowers of exquisite trumpet-shape. It is deliciously fragrant.

If you go to the Savill Gardens in early spring you may see one of the great sights of

Nomocharis pardanthina

horticulture; there must be millions of *Narcissus bulbocodium citrinus* naturalised in the moist grassy meadow. They are known as Hoop Petticoat daffodils on account of their intriguing shape, and will seed themselves in marshy ground. Likewise at Wisley, on the alpine meadow *N. bulbocodium* itself, richer yellow than *citrinus*, is just as prolific. The ground in both gardens, where they grow, is oozy wet and this is the secret of success. If sown from seeds they will take about five years to reach flowering size.

At Rowallane in Northern Ireland I came across some clumps of *Narcissus moschatus* 'Plenus'. It was at one time called *N. cernuus* 'Plenus', which name indicates its nodding habit. I love the single flowers of the species, but have a warm spot in my heart for this delectable double-flowered form. They are not just many petalled; the doubling is *only within the trumpet* and is most appealing. The colour is creamy white and the stems reach about ten inches. I find it quite happy in any fertile soil and it increases fairly freely. It is now classed as a variety of *N. pseudonarcissus*.

There are times when I long for cool moist woodland conditions in my garden. One of the first things I should try to grow would be the species of *Nomocharis*, those bulbous lily-like charmers which do so well at the Royal Botanic Garden, Edinburgh. They are easy to raise from seeds, and when well suited are good perennials achieving about three feet. I know no plants—not even lilies themselves—that have such an air of breeding, each flower a slightly nodding miracle of loveliness with six segments, often with fringed

Paradisea liliastrum

edges. Of delicate pink, they are mostly spotted with crimson. Words of mine do not do justice to their ethereal beauty.

Known in our gardens for centuries is St Bruno's Lily, *Paradisea liliastrum*, beautiful and yet little known. It is often confused with St Bernard's Lily which we have already looked at under *Anthericum*. St Bruno's has similar foliage, grey-green and rather limp, but the flowers are considerably larger. It has no scent to speak of, but is of a crystalline whiteness good to behold. It is best to plant the fleshy roots in autumn, in any fertile soil, so that they can gather strength for flowering in early summer, along with the first peonies.

My next plant, *Puya alpestris*, was splendid at Mount Stewart, Northern Ireland, where it enjoys the soft climate. It also grows and flowers well at Clevedon Court, Avon, but is not reliably hardy just anywhere in England. It should be given a warm sunny position in fast-draining soil. Then, after a number of years of preparation it will present you over its tough pointed leaves a spire of blossom unlike anything else out-of-doors. The flowers are satiny, of an incredible peacock blue-green, lit by orange stamens. It is said that the elongated extremities of flowering branches, which carry no flowers, are used as perches by birds in search of nectar, with which the flowers are generously provided, and thereby aid pollination. Despite its striking appearance I doubt whether this puya will ever be common in cultivation. Raised from seeds, as it was when first brought from Chile prior to 1869, a flowering stem may be expected in about five years.

Puya alpestris (left and above)

From South Africa comes the splendid red Kaffir Lily, *Schizostylis coccinea*—not a lily at all, but belonging to the Iris Family. Like so many of our garden plants from South Africa it needs moist soil in a sunny position to hasten its flowers, which seldom appear before September. The plant, introduced in 1864, from which the species was described, had small crocuslike, rich crimson flowers all up a stem of about two feet over grassy foliage. It has sported in cultivation and in the wild to various pink tints, and my favourite is 'Sunrise', which flourishes at Hidcote, Gloucestershire. It was raised about 1970 by The Plantsmen, and is a sturdy and prolific grower. But to be a success it *must* have moist soil in full sun, when it will go on flowering until the frosts stop it. These plants are some of the best for keeping the summer flag flying until all is over.

Another plant which, though introduced in 1640, has never become popular, is *Smilacina racemosa*, a native of North America. It needs cool moist soil preferably without lime, and is seen doing well at Wisley, Surrey, throwing up its elegant leafy stems, so like those of Solomon's Seal (in its native land it is called False Solomon's Seal) but with a tuft of fragrant flowers at the top, in early summer. Because of its early awakening in spring it

Schizostylis coccinea 'Sunrise'

Smilacina racemosa

is best to plant the tuberous roots, only a few inches down, in autumn. It is long-lived, and in some seasons red berries mature in autumn over the yellowing leaves.

Stenanthium robustum is seldom seen. It came to us from the United States in 1813, and although it bears little resemblance to a lily, yet it is of that Family. When suited in cool moist soil, the tuberous roots throw up tall stems bearing multitudes of creamy white stars, rather after the style of the veratrums, but smaller. At Mount Stewart, Northern Ireland, it thrives in well drained, humus-rich soil in broken sunlight. It should be planted in early autumn and left severely alone. It requires several years to flower from seeds.

Most of us want to grow trilliums, but it is no use attempting them unless you have semi-woodland conditions on moist, humus-laden, lime-free soil. They thrive at the Botanic Garden in Edinburgh, though they thrive also at Wisley and at the Savill Gardens. As long ago as 1759 *Trillium erectum* was brought from eastern North America, where it has acquired the strange names of Squaw Root and Stinking Benjamin. In this and all species

Stenanthium robustum

Trillium erectum

Trillium grandiflorum 'Plenum'

Trillium grandiflorum

Trillium grandiflorum 'Roseum'

the parts of the leaves and flowers are, as the name of *Trillium* suggests, in threes—three leaves, three sepals, three petals, three stamens, etcetera. They are all beautiful long-lived plants so long as their needs are studied. *T. erectum* has flowers of brownish purple; there are also white, yellow, and green forms. By far the best known, and prolific of increase of its tuberous roots, is *T. grandiflorum*. It came to us at the end of the 18th century and has been well known ever since. Furthermore it has developed some really delectable forms which are much treasured by those who are fortunate to possess them. They include one of clear rose-pink tint and a double white which has the perfect form of a camellia. In this species I have noticed marked variation in the size and quality of the flowers, and urge you always to see your plant in flower before purchasing.

It is noticeable that people (by which of course I mean gardeners) are always ready to welcome the first of any genus to flower, while I suppose a kind of boredom sets in which destroys their interest in the late-flowering species or varieties. This is what has happened I think with *Tulipa sprengeri*, though the neglect may simply be due to the fact that it flowers after tulips have contributed so splendidly to the annual spring bedding, and therefore there is no need to bother with a late tulip. Whatever may be the cause of *T. sprengeri* being so little grown, it is a sad fact because we therefore deny ourselves a great beauty. After all, there is no real excuse for the neglect; it has been in our gardens, from Asia Minor, since 1894, and I find it a true perennial, increasing itself by seed. The stem and leaves are rich green and the flowers a glowing tomato-red, paler outside, and of a neat and slender shape. The seed pods mature well, produce plenty of seeds, and are ornamental when dried. I find it thrives in the rather cooler positions, though I have seen it growing well in a sunny bed at Oxford University Botanic Garden—limy and gravelly,

Tulipa sprengeri

Uvularia grandiflora

Veratrum album

Veratrum nigrum

just the opposite of my soil. All this points to the fact that it is a plant easy to manage. Why should it be so scarce and expensive?

Also from North America, whence it arrived in 1802, is *Uvularia grandiflora*, another relative of the Solomon's Seal, though this time shorter and with dangling light yellow flowers somewhat hidden under the fresh green leafy shoots. It is a spring charmer for any cool spot, with humus, preferably without lime.

Veratrum album, a member of the Lily Family, has great fleshy roots that take kindly to heavy soil. It is known as the False or White Helleborine, though I must add that it is difficult to see the connection with the hellebores. All the veratrums need rich deep soil, and unless sheltered from wind their foliage, which is handsome, broad and pleated in spring, will look tatty by flowering time, which is midsummer. *V. nigrum* has tall spikes of dark chocolate-maroon stars, while the shorter *V. viride* is a study in green. Though they lack floral *éclat* they are always noticed in the garden, being tall and reliably erect. They can be divided in autumn if necessary but I should avoid it if possible; they will take at least two years to recover. *V. nigrum* came from Europe and Siberia in the 16th century and *V. viride* arived from North America in the late 18th century.

Veratrum viride

An apology should probably be given for including two yuccas in this book of perennials. While woody-stemmed they can scarcely be called shrubs. They are something all on their own and deserve close attention. *Yucca filifera*, once called *Y. flaccida*, is almost herbaceous, its leaves are evergreen, of hard leathery texture, and give rise to flowering stems about every third year. It is always a great thrill to see the knobbly bud in the centre of the leaf-rosette maturing, to give rise to a stem some four feet high hung with glistening starry bells of cream. In southeastern United States, where this yucca is native, the sweet lemon scent attracts night-flying moths that deposit their eggs while pollinating the flowers.

In *Yucca* 'Vittorio Emmanuele II', on the other hand, we have a little-known hybrid that grows large, and might well be called a shrub. The stems reach to three or four feet on top of which are grouped masses of spiky leaves; it is reputedly a hybrid of *Y. aloifolia purpurea* raised in 1901. It imitates some of the latter's warm colouring in the buds on the

Yucca filifera

Yucca 'Vittorio Emmanuele II'

Zantedeschia aethiopica 'Crowborough'

Zygadenus elegans

massive spikes of creamy bells. Flowers are produced fairly regularly and appear in their glory in the summer months, not in autumn when those of the similar *Y. gloriosa* so often succumb to frost. Groups of 'Vittorio Emmanuele II' terminate the sunny borders at Polesden Lacey, Surrey, and they give a magnificent effect, flowering in most years.

The so-called Arum Lily of our greenhouses is a native of South Africa and needs a lot of moisture to thrive. Both the foliage of dark shining green and the magnificent creamy white sculptured flowers always command attention. Many years ago I was told about a great row of them in a garden at Crowborough, Sussex, growing in the open without protection. I went to the garden and was overcome by the magnificent sight. The result was that I came away with some roots that were the start of the form which now goes under the name of *Zantedeschia aethiopica* 'Crowborough'. I have since come across other apparently hardy arums. Whether these are upland forms of the species and can therefore withstand cooler and drier conditions has yet to be proved; I have never had the space and patience to try the greenhouse plants outside. I have had them in heavy and sandy soils with equal success, but find the 'Crowborough' form not hardy until its great root-fangs get well down into the soil. There is no doubt that this superb plant need not be thoughtlessly relegated to greenhouses, to provide cut-bloom for church festivals. It can be an ornament of great quality out of doors as well. It is strange that a plant first known to us in 1731 should earn its rightful place in the garden only recently. It is best planted deeply in spring and provided with plenty of moisture during the growing season.

A charming member of the Lily Family from North America, *Zigadenus elegans*, has been in our gardens since 1828 but remains little known. Perhaps its lack of popularity is due to its subdued colouring, for it is hardy and easy to cultivate in any fertile soil, in sun or part shade, limy or acid, so long as there is some moisture. Its foliage, narrow and grassy, and its stems and buds have a greyish tinge from the many small hairs and scales. But it is the flowers that elevate it from the commonplace. The stems reach to about two feet bearing numerous, cupshaped starry flowers, small but exquisite in pale creamy green. I can think of few plants with more charm, but its impact comes with the second glance. The fleshy, thong-like roots can be planted in spring or autumn, but not where children might be tempted to taste it. Most zygadenes contain unpleasant alkaloids and a common name for all of them in their native land is Death Camas. The more widely grown veratrums have similar alkaloids yet retain their popularity with gardeners.

Dactylorhiza elata

PART FIVE

Hardy Orchids

The plum broke forth in green,
   The pear stood high and snowed,
My friends and I between
   Would take the Ludlow road;
Dressed to the nines and drinking
   And light in heart and limb,
And each chap thinking
   The fair was held for him.

Last Poems, xxxiv, A. E. Housman

I t strikes me as little short of extraordinary that so many plants should have been in cultivation in these islands for so many years—even hundreds of years—without ever becoming popular. In a way it is a blessing because it gives us something to do, to evaluate them and work them into our planting schemes. Some of the plants in earlier pages could well become popular, others will need a lot of pushing if they are ever to hit the headlines. The popular plants of today are, many of them, the results of hybridising a limited few species in each genus. Take for instance phloxes, irises, poppies, erigerons, peonies: all the popular strains have been developed from just two or three species with no thought to the widely varied other species that could have influenced the hybrids immeasurably. This is possibly one reason for the conundrum; another may be that these popular strains have had a lot of publicity and in the days when ordering plants was left to the head gardener, perhaps he did not look far enough. In any case it was the effect of flowers that was sought, whereas I like to think it is the effect of the plants that is now uppermost in our minds. Today it is not enough to appraise the flowers, we have to look and study the whole plant if each garden is to be different from the next.

My choices for these pages have been made arbitrarily from among the less popular plants. I hope that those selected have brought home the general difference between the

Dicots, with their great diversity in foliage, and the Monocots, many of which have plain grassy or strap shaped leaves (apart from the Aroids, where many are lobed and net veined, and the embryos of even these plants have but one cotyledon.)

Now let us look at the orchids. I have deliberately left them for a separate little chapter though they are also Monocots. They are so rarified that I felt they deserved a section to themselves. I was brought up in Cambridge and I remember as a boy going with my parents to woods and fields where cowslips and oxlips grew accompanied by orchids. We used to call them *Orchis* in those days; now they are *Dactylorhiza*, but they have the same enchantment. Johns' *Flowers of the Field* was on our bookshelves at home, which enabled a deal of sorting to be done. It so happened that in my early years the *Boys' Own Paper* had a serial running called The Orchid Hunters; so far as I recall it was concerned with discovering exotic species in the forests of Borneo. It seems to me that this was a surprising serial served up in a periodical journal mainly devoted to the excitements of youth. But there is no doubt that for me it put orchids on a top shelf from which they have never descended. At about the same time a friend at school in Norfolk brought me tins of *Orchis morio*, *O. mascula*, and others from The Lows, near Holt. These I grew in my father's garden where I had a small patch of my own. By the time I was seventeen I had made a bed of peat in which I grew successfully *Cypripedium reginae* and *C. calceolus* (with lime). From then onwards I have never been without orchids of some sort.

I had read about *Bletilla striata* for many years, and that it needed peat and coolness to thrive, but I had never grown it. Judge of my surprise therefore to find it growing in a narrow border at the foot of a greenhouse at Kew facing south, in full sunshine, flowering freely and increasing wildly. I was given some spare roots and they grew well in a similar position in my own garden, but did not produce flowers, much to my disappointment. Its pleated bright green leaves form a good setting for the stems each bearing several narrow flowers, and lasting well. In addition to the usual pink, the species has produced forms with white and pale pink flowers. It is a native of China and was first grown in our gardens in 1802, when it was known as *Bletia hyacinthina*. The tuberous roots are best planted shallowly in early autumn.

The cypripediums are the most sought after of hardy orchids. The species grown for many years in greenhouses have now been transferred to other genera, so the hardy ones reign supreme. Of the dozen or more species from around the northern Temperate Zone—especially in North America and eastern Asia, with a few in Europe—none is more stalwart and beautiful than *Cypripedium reginae*, formerly known as *C. spectabile*. It hails from the United States and reached our gardens in the early 18th century. The old pictures of it are full of the wonderment due to the most handsome of all orchids that can be grown in the open ground. And it is not difficult to grow providing you start with good fresh roots and give them a cool moist position in lime-free soil in a humus laden mixture. The white guard petals stand behind a rosy pouch of wonderful beauty. *C. calceolus* is a study in

Bletilla striata

Cypripedium reginae

yellow and rich red-brown. *C. candidum* from North America echoes it in white and brown. Other species from Asia give us pink and mauve flowers. There is no end to the delectation. But I must add a word of warning. All plants sold are collected in the wild, which is likely in time to render all species extinct, as happened with *C. calceolus* in Britain where it was at one time common.* Therefore until their propagation from seeds has been investigated and found to be a practical proposition we should not purchase them. So much has been done for other genera in the way of propagation that I venture to hope that the time is not far distant when young nursery-grown plants may become available.

The species of *Dactylorhiza* include several that are amenable and increase freely in cultivation, provided their simple needs are met. I have had no trouble in growing several species in my acid-soil garden, where they take their chance with other plants and increase freely. They are best split up in early autumn, or at any time before spring, planting them at strictly the same depth in soil well mixed with humus. A spectacular patch of *D. elata* could once be seen at Sissinghurst—perhaps is there still. There is no doubt of their garden value when seen in the mass, though a solitary spike will usually bring forth an exclamation from those unacquainted with it. I have had equal success with *D. majalis majalis*, which is a shade paler and a bit later, with distinctively spotted leaves. *D. foliosa*, rather taller, is later still and flowers with the plant of unknown origin that we call 'Glasnevin', after the famous Dublin garden where it was first seen. Then there is *D. fuchsii* which is a taller variant of equal charm. They are all great treasures which present little difficulty. I have not been so successful with *D. mascula* and *D. morio* both of which I think prefer almost boggy conditions in limy soil. Though I consider the lifting of orchids from the wild a reprehensible act, I hope I may be pardoned for having lifted a few *D. mascula* from a Cotswold meadow where the cows were rapidly driving them into the marshy ground.

*It has now been re-established from colonies of plants raised at Kew Gardens.

Alstroemeria ligtu hybrids

PART SIX

Music

When lads were home from labour
    At Abdon under Clee,
A man would call his neighbour
    And both would send for me.
And when the light in lances
    Across the mead was laid,
There to the dances
    I fetched my flute and played.

Last Poems, XLI, A. E. Housman

As the years roll by certain memories fade, others remain clear-cut while the future becomes increasing nebulous in its uncertainty. I have written earlier how lucky I was to have been born in the fair city—or town as it then was—of Cambridge. I want now to set down a few points about my home and how they affected my life.

There was always beauty in my home. Good furniture, carpets, pictures, mostly chosen by my father; a well designed little garden, also my father's, and many lovely plants grown by my mother. Indoors was her embroidery and music: she taught at one time the piano and other subjects to a family in Belgium. She was an expert pianist. My father had been a choirboy and in later life sang tenor with several organizations including the Cambridge Philharmonic Society and the Cambridge University Musical Society. Of course I went to concerts—in King's College Chapel and the Guildhall—in which he took part, and thus at an early age was getting familiar with Bach, Handel, Mendelssohn, Brahms, Honegger, Delius and other composers. My mother's favourite compositions for the piano were those of Chopin and Beethoven.

There were other musical events to attend, such as the annual madrigal singing on the Cam, the banks along The Backs lined with listeners. For the last madrigal Japanese lanterns were inserted in the raft of joined punts and the singers floated downstream singing Wilbye's immortal *Draw on Sweet Night*, often accompanied by quacking ducks. And one year a Pageant of British Music was given in the open air by the west door of King's College Chapel, starting with *Summer is icumen in*, madrigals and part songs. The pageant ended with the arrival of the great Handel himself.

During the singing one evening rain started to fall. As many of the concourse as were able crammed themselves into the great Victorian dining hall of King's College where the programme continued. The comparatively confined space led to new appreciation of the English Madrigal. The words and the music made a definite impression on my ears though the river, sky, trees and buildings were absent. I resolved there and then that one of my ambitions in life was to sing these musical masterpieces of the 16th and 17th centuries, the like of which have never been repeated.

Some years after my arrival in Surrey the opportunity occurred. A number of friends joined together for carol singing at Christmas; there were several expert singers and musicians. Among the good causes for which we sang was the Woking hospital. This all led to my searching for some special carols that would lighten the collection of old favourites. And then in the New Year we decided to go on singing together, choosing part songs and madrigals, and after rehearsing for a few weeks we would put on a performance in one of our houses or the village hall in aid of a worthy cause. The meetings started afresh after the Second World War but carols and part songs were left behind and we concentrated on English madrigals. We were fortunate in attracting some gifted conductors from time to time and reached sufficient skill to compete in the Woking Music Festival, where we won good marks. After a time we gave up singing for good causes and relaxed into once-monthly singing in members' houses, simply for our own enjoyment of this period music.

Woking was quite a musical place as well as being the centre of the Surrey nurseries. There was the Woking Music Club, which ran concerts of celebrities among whom were great singers such as Stuart Robertson and Eric Greene. It was a coincidence I suppose that at the time I had become enthused by the poems of A. E. Housman, for in those inter-war years settings of Housman's poems by such master composers as Vaughan Williams, Gurney, Butterworth and others were very popular. This fact seems to point to my adoption of Housman for my own settings of three of his poems and my use here of his lines as epigraphs.

It is one thing to be fond of music but quite another to be sufficiently adept to be able to play and sing. Desirous of singing in the Woking Choral Society, I took singing lessons from Mrs Margaret Walker, the conductor of the Society and a person of boundless enthusiasm and ability. This enabled me to sing tenor in such works as the *B minor Mass*, Brahms' *Requiem*, Fauré's *Requiem*, the *St John's Passion* and Parry's *Songs of Farewell*.

My three songs owe not a little to the enthusiasm of Margaret Walker and also to Humphrey Hare, who taught chemistry at Leighton Park School at Reading, though he was also expert at the piano, organ, 'cello and singing. I had met both him and John Gilmour at botany lectures at Cambridge. John I linked up with again later when he became Director of the Royal Horticultural Society's Garden at Wisley.

The fact that I had a voice drove me on to sing a variety of songs principally because a friend, Mary Jones, of Woking, was a pianist of consummate skill and artistry. Without her I doubt whether I should have been able to tackle several Schumann song cycles, some fifty Brahms' Lieder, a few of Richard Strauss', besides a considerable number of traditional and comparatively new British songs by such maestros as Vaughan Williams, Warlock, Quilter, Somervell, and also by Bach, Handel, Purcell and others.

Having spent many years in lodgings I eventually acquired a house of my own. With it was my mother's piano. An old friend, Mrs A. T. Johnson, in North Wales, bequeathed me her upright Bluthner piano so that two-piano duets were now possible. Several friends enjoyed coming along, including of course Mary Jones. But I was no gifted pianist though I flatter myself I had "touch". I had to *learn* piano pieces, and songs. One day I asked Mary where she was reading the notes which she was playing. She said "two or three bars ahead". This made me realise that however much I practised I should never be any good and I gave up work on the piano forthwith. I have been told that sight-reading "comes with practice". All I can say is that I practised for over fifty years and it never came to me. But even so music has given a great deal of pleasure during my life. I think that music and gardening make good companions; they bring into use different senses and abilities and together make for happy days.

My three songs owe their being to Housman's simple and evocative poems about flowers and I offer them with all diffidence. The flowers of course come first, and here they are. The fair copies were made by my old friend Philip Irwin and to him I tender my best thanks.

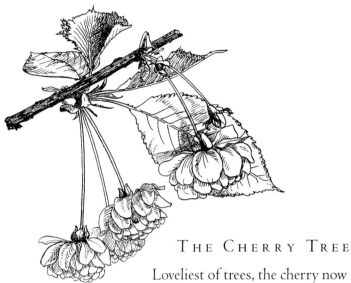

THE CHERRY TREE

Loveliest of trees, the cherry now
Is hung with bloom along the bough,
And stands about the woodland ride
Wearing white for Eastertide.

Now, of my threescore years and ten,
Twenty will not come again,
And take from seventy springs a score,
It only leaves me fifty more.

And since to look at things in bloom
Fifty springs are little room,
About the woodlands I will go
To see the cherry hung with snow.

From *A Shropshire Lad*, 11, by A. E. Housman

Line drawing of *Prunus avium* 'Plena' by the author.

The Cherry Tree

bout the wood-land I will go. To see the Cher-ry hung with snow

THE GOLDEN BROOM

'Tis time, I think, by Wenlock town
The golden broom should blow;
The hawthorn sprinkled up and down
Should charge the land with snow.

Spring will not wait the loiterer's time
Who keeps so long away;
So others wear the broom and climb
The hedgerows heaped with may.

Oh tarnish late on Wenlock Edge,
Gold that I never see;
Lie long, high snowdrifts in the hedge
That will not shower on me.

Into my heart an air that kills
From yon far country blows:
What are those blue remembered hills,
What spires, what farms are those?

That is the land of lost content,
I see it shining plain,
The happy highways where I went
And cannot come again.

    From *A Shropshire Lad*, XXXIX & XL,
    by A. E. Housman

Line drawing of *Cytisus scoparium* by the author.

The Golden Broom

Dreamily

'Tis time I think by Wen-lock town The gol-den broom should blow; The haw-thorn sprin-kled up and down Should charge the land with snow. Spring will not wait the loi-terer's time who keeps so long a-way; So o-thers wear the

THE LENT LILY

'Tis spring; come out to ramble
The hilly brakes around,
For under thorn and bramble
About the hollow ground
The primroses are found.

And there's the windflower chilly
With all the winds at play,
And there's the Lenten lily
That has not long to stay
And dies on Easter day.

And since till girls go maying
You find the primrose still,
And find the windflower playing
With every wind at will,
But not the daffodil,

Bring baskets now, and sally
Upon the spring's array,
And bear from hill and valley
The daffodil away
That dies on Easter day.

From *A Shropshire Lad*, XXIX,
by A. E. Housman

Line drawing of *Narcissus pseudonarcissus* by the author.

The Lent Lily

With the great gale we journey
That breathes from gardens thinned,
Borne in the drift of blossoms
Whose petals throng the wind;

Buoyed on the heaven-heard whisper
Of dancing leaflets whirled
From all the woods that Autumn
Bereaves in all the world.

From *A Shropshire Lad*, XLII,
by A. E. Housman

GENERAL INDEX

Arends, Georg, 17
Arnott, Mr, 104

Ballard, Helen, 42
Bloom, Alan, 76, 101
Bowles, E. A., 41, 89
Bressingham Gardens, Norfolk, 110
Burtt, B. L., 30, 64

Chatto, Beth, 69, 83, 108, 116
Chelsea Flower Show, xiii
Chiltern Hills, xii
Christchurch, Hampshire, 24
Cooke, Mr R. B., 55

Delavay, Abbé, 44
Dicotyledonous plants, xiv

Farrer, Reginald, 54, 69, 118
Findlay, Hope, 93
Fish, Margery, 15, 35
Fortescue, Lionel, 69
Frikart, of Switzerland, 17

Gray, Alec, 123
Greene, Eric, 144

Halliwell, Brian, 30
Hancock, James, 15
Hare, Humphrey, 145
Housman, A. E., xi, xiv, 1, 9, 83, 91, 139, 143, 144, 146,
    150, 154, 157
Hurst, Dr C. C., xiii

Jekyll, Gertrude, 22, 50, 64
Johnson, A. T., 26
Johnson, Nora (Mrs A. T.), 145
Jones, Mary, 145

Kelway, Messrs, of Somerset, 57
Klehm, Messrs, of Illinois, 57

Ladhams, Ernest, 24
Lawley, Frank, 45
Lemoine, Messrs, of Nancy, 17, 58, 101

Marshall, Nigel, 29
Mason, Maurice, 63
Maurice Prichard & Sons, 39
Monocotyledonous plants, xiv
Moore, Hugh Armitage, 72
Moore, Lady (Phylis), 9, 15, 108
Moreton, Oscar, 29, 30
Muir, Mrs J. B., 84, 120

Palmer, Lewis, 93
Pitt, William, 29
Prichard, Maurice, 24

Robertson, Stuart, 144
Robinson, William, 22, 77

Saunders, Dr A. P., 57, 58
Saunders, Miss, xiii
Savill Gardens, Berkshire, 123, 124
Schilling, A. D. (Tony), 37, 98, 106
Seward, A. C., xiii
Sheldon, Mr, 52
Smith, Eric, 98, 108
St Christopher, 10
Stern, Sir Frederick, 42, 115, 118
Symons-Jeune, Captain B. H. B., 76

Treasure's Nursery, Herefordshire, 25

Walker, Margaret (Mrs), 145
Ward, Kingdon, 52
Wisley Garden, Surrey, 124

Zauschner, Professor, 33

INDEX OF PLANTS

Numbers in the left-hand column indicate the hardiness zones illustrated on the map on pages 168 and 169; numbers in boldface type refer to illustrations.

7–9	*Acanthus dioscoridis*, 9		4–8	*nemorosa*, Wood Anemone, 13
7–10	*mollis*, 9			'Lismore Pink', 13
7–9	*perringii*, 9			'Vestal', **13**
6–10	*spinosus*, 9			'Prinz Heinrich' ('Prince Henry'), 12
	'Lady Moore', **10**		4–8	*ranunculoides*, 13
5–8	*Aconitum napellus*, Monkshood, 10		6–8	*rivularis*, 14
	'Album Grandiflorum', **10**		5–8	× *seemannii* (*A.* × *lipsiensis*), 14
	'Carneum', 10, **11**			*sulfurea*. See *Pulsatilla alpina apiifolia*
	Actaea, Baneberry, 10, 24		5–8	*vitifolia*, 12
3–9	*alba*, 10		7–9	*Anthericum algeriense*, 95, 125
4–9	*spicata*, Herb Christopher, 10		6–9	*liliago* 'Major', **95**
	Adiantum, Maidenhair Fern, 2		5–9	*Aralia racemosa*, 14, **15**
3–8	*pedatum*, 2, **3**		5–8	*Artemisia absinthium*, Wormwood, 15
	'Japonicum', 3		8–9	*arborescens*, 15
2–8	*subpumilum*, 3		5–8	*canescens*, 15
4–8	*venustum*, 2		5–8	'Powis Castle', 15, **16**
9–10	*Agapanthus* 'Alice Gloucester', 93		5–8	*vallesiaca*, 15, **16**
	africanus, 93		8–9	*Arum creticum*, **95**
8–10	*campanulatus*, 93			Arum Lily. See *Zantedeschia aethiopica*
	'Cherry Holley', 93			*Arundo conspicua*. See *Chionochloa conspicua*
	'Loch Hope', **92**, 93		7–10	*donax* 'Variegata', 83, **84**
3–7	*Alchemilla mollis*, 63		6–8	*Asphodeline lutea*, King's Spear, 96
4–8	*Allium* (Onion) *aflatunense*, 93		5–8	*Aster* × *frikartii*, 8, 17
	albopilosum. See *A. christophii*			'Eiger', 17
4–8	*christophii*, **93**			'Jungfrau', 17
4–8	*karataviense*, **93**, 94			'Mönch', 17
7–10	*Alstroemeria aurantiaca*, 94		5–9	*thompsonii*, 17
7–10	*haemantha*, 94		4–9	*Astilbe astilboides*, 17
7–10	*ligtu*, **94**, 95, **142**		3–8	*davidii*, 17
4–8	*Anemone* × *hybrida*, Japanese anemone, 12		4–9	'Etna', **18**
	'Honorine Jobert', **12**		4–8	*japonica*, 17
5–8	*hupehensis japonica*, 12		4–8	*tacquetii*, 17
	var. *japonica*, 12			'Jo Ophorst', 19
5–8	*narcissiflora*, **14**			'Purpurlanz', 19

4–8   *thunbergii*, 17
            'Betsy Cuperus', 17
            'Ostrich Plume', 17, **18**
4–8   'Professor van der Wielen', 17

4–9   *Baptisia australis*, 19
6–9   *Begonia grandis* (*B. evansiana*), 19, **20**
        Bignonia. See *Campsis*
5–8   *Blechnum*, 2, 3
        Bletia hyacinthina. See *Bletilla striata*
6–9   *Bletilla striata*, 140, **141**
        Blue African Lilies. See *Agapanthus*
        Burning Bush. See *Dictamnus*

        California Tree Poppy. See *Romneya coulteri*
        Camassia, 96
5–9   'Eve Price', 96
5–9   *leichtlinii*, 96
                'Electra', **97**, 98
                'Plena', **97**, 98
4–8   *Campanula* × *burghaltii*, 20
4–8   *punctata*, 19–20, **21**
10–11   *vidalii*, **ii**, iv
5–9   *Campsis*, Trumpet Vine, 44
        Cape Figwort. See *Phygelius*
5–9   *Cardamine heptaphylla*, **20**
6–8   *Cardiocrinum giganteum*, **98**
        Carnation. *See* Clove carnation
        Cathcartia villosa. See *Meconopsis villosa*
7–9   *Cautleya*, 99
            'Robusta', **99**
4–8   *Centaurea* 'Pulchra Major'. See *Leuzea*
                centaurioides
7–10   *Chionochloa conspicua*, **84**
        Christmas Fern. See *Polystichum acrostichoides*
                and *Polystichum munitum*
        Chrysanthemum, 20
4–9   'Emperor of China', **22**
5–9   *nipponicum*, 22, **23**
            old cottage pink. See *Chrysanthemum*
                'Emperor of China'
3–8   *Cimicifuga foetida*, 23, **24**
4–8   *racemosa*, **24**
4–8   *ramosa*, 23
3–8   *simplex*, 24
                'Elstead Variety', 24
                'Prichard's Giant', 24
                'White Pearl', 24

5–7   *Clematis douglasii scottiae*, 25
            hirsutissima scottiae, **25**
4–8   Clove carnation, 27
            'Earl of Chatham', 29
            Old Salmon Clove, 29
            'Phyllis Marshall', 29
            'Raby Castle', 29
7–9   *Cortaderia*, 84
7–9   *fulvida*, 84, **85**
9–10   *jubata*, 89
7–9   *richardii*, Toe-toe Grass, 84, **85**
7–9   *selloana*, Pampas Grass, 84, 87, 89
                'Monstrosa', **86**, 87
                'Pumila', **87**, 89
                'Rendatleri', **86**, 87
                'Sunningdale Silver', **82**, 87
5–7   *Corydalis lutea*, 25
5–7   *nobilis*, 25
5–7   *ochroleuca*, 25
        Cowslip. See *Primula veris*
5–7   *Crepis incana*, 26
7–9   *Crinum* × *powellii*, 99
            'Album', 99
            'Haarlemense', 99, **100**, 101
5–9   *Crocosmia* × *crocosmiiflora*, 101
            'Carmin Brillant', **100**, 101
            'Vesuvius', 101
        Crucianella stylosa. See *Phuopsis stylosa*
2–8   *Cryptogamma*, 3
        Cypripedium, 140–141
3–7   *calceolus*, 140, 141
6–8   *candidum*, 141
3–7   *reginae*, 140, **141**
5–8   *spectabile*, 140
6–8   *Cytisus scoparium*, **150**

        Dactylorhiza, 140, 141
7–9   *elata*, **138**, 141
5–8   *fuchsii*, 141
7–9   'Glasnevin', 141
5–8   *majalis majalis*, 141
5–8   *mascula*, 141
5–8   *morio*, 141
        Danthonia conspicua. See *Chionochloa conspicua*
6–8   *Darmera peltata* (*Peltiphyllum peltatum*), 26, **27**
        Delphinium, 26
6–7   *nudicaule*, 27, **28**
8–9   *wellbyi*, 27, **28**

Dendranthema. See *Chrysanthemum*

Dentaria pinnata. See *Cardamine heptaphylla*

4—8 Dianthus 'Old Clove', **29**

8—9 Diascia fetcaniensis, 30

7—9 rigescens, 30, **31**

6—8 Dicentra chrysantha, **30**

9—10 Dicksonia, 2

 Dictamnus, Burning Bush, 33

2—8 albus, **32**, 33

   'Purpureus', **32**

 Dierama, 101, 102

7—9 dracomontanum, 101

7—9 pendulum, 101

7—9 pulcherrimum, Wand Flower, Venus' Fishing Rod, **100**, 101

 Dittany. See *Dictamnus*, Burning Bush

4—8 Dryopteris affinis, xviii

4—8 pseudomas (*D. borreri*), 3, 5

4—8 wallichiana, **4**, 5

8—10 Elder. See *Sambucus*

8—10 Epilobium canum, **33**, 34

5—8 Erodium, 37

 Eryngium, Sea Holly, 34

3—10 alpinum, **34**

8—10 proteiflorum, **34**

   'Delaroux', 34

 Erythronium, 102

2—7 dens-canis, 102

4—8 'Pagoda', **102**

8—10 Eucomis pallidiflora, 103

 Euphorbia, 35—37

7—9 characias, 35

   'John Tomlinson', 35

   'Lambrook Gold', 35

   var. *sibthorpii*, **35**

7—9 wulfenii, 35

6—8 myrsinites, 35, **36**

5—9 palustris, 35, **36**

6—8 schillingii, **36**, 37

6—9 wallichii, **36**, 37

 Fair Maids of France. See *Ranunculus aconitifoluius*

7—10 Fatsia, 14

4—8 Filipendula palmata, 'Rubra', **37**

4—8 purpurea 'Elegans', 37

Fritillaria libanotica. See *F. persica*

4—8 meleagris, Snake's Head Lily, 103

5—8 pallidiflora, 103

6—8 persica 'Adiyaman', **90**, 104

 Galanthus, 104

4—8 'Beth Chatto', 104

4—8 'Cicely Hall', 104

4—8 'Mighty Atom', 104

4—8 'S. Arnott', 104

 Geranium, 37

4—8 endressii, 39

4—8 pratense, Meadow Cranesbill, 37, 38

   'Plenum Album', 38

   'Plenum Caeruleum', 38

   'Plenum Violaceum', **38**

4—8 × riversleaianum, 38

   'Mavis Simpson', **39**

   'Russell Prichard', 39, **40**

8—9 traversii, 39

4—8 wallichianum 'Syabru', 39

6—9 Glaucidium palmatum, 39, **41**

   leucanthum, 41

7—10 Habranthus pratensis, 107

 Harebell Poppy. See *Meconopsis quintuplinervia*

 Hedychium, 104—106

7—10 densiflorum 'Tara', 106

7—10 gardnerianum, 104, **105**

6—8 Helleborus argutifolius (*H. lividus corsicus*), 42

5—9 atrorubens, 41

6—9 cyclophyllus, 42

5—9 kochii, 41

   'Bowles' Yellow', 41, 42

7—9 lividus, **42**, 43

4—7 niger, 41, 43

4—9 orientalis, 41, 42

6—9 × sternii, 42

 Hemerocallis, Day Lily, 106—107

3—10 fulva, 107

3—10   var. *rosea*, **106**

3—10 'J. S. Gaynor', **106**

3—10 'Kwanso Flore Pleno', 107

3—10 'Kwanso Variegata', **107**

3—10 'Missenden', 107

 Herb Christopher. See *Actaea spicata*

4—9 Hesperis matronalis, Sweet Rocket, Dame's Violet, 43

5–8   *Hieracium lanatum*, **43**
5–8   *waldsteinii*, 43
9–10 *Hippeastrum pratense*, **107**
      Hosta, 107–110
3–9   *fortunei* 'Albopicta', **108**
3–9   'Frances Williams', 108, **109**
3–9   'Halcyon', 108, **109**
3–9   *plantaginea* 'Aphrodite', 107
3–9   *tokudama* 'Aureonebulosa', 108, **110**
3–9   'White Colossus', **110**
5–8   *Hylomecon japonicum*, 43

5–8   *Incarvillea delavayi*, **44**
      grandiflora brevipes. See *I. mairei*
5–8   *mairei*, 44, **45**
        'Bees Pink', 44
        'Frank Ludlow', 44
        'Nyoto Sama', 44
7–8   *olgae*, 66
4–8   *Inula oculis-christi*, 45, **46**
4–9   *Iris ensata*, 110
4–9   'Gracchus', 113, **114**
6–9   *kerneriana*, 45, **113**
4–9   *laevigata*, 110, **112**
        'Variegata', **111**
4–9   'Mlle Yvonne Pellitier', **113**, 114
6–9   'Ochraurea', 113
6–9   *orientalis*, 113
6–9   *pallida* 'Variegata', 110, **111**
5–9   *pseudacorus* 'Variegata', 110, **111**
7–9   *tingitana fontanesii*, **114**, 115

      Japanese anemone. See *Anemone × hybrida*
5–7   *Jeffersonia diphylla*, 46
5–8   *dubia*, **46**

      Kaffir Lily. See *Schizostylis coccinea*
5–8   *Kirengeshoma palmata*, 46, **47**
      Kniphofia, Red Hot Poker, 115–116
6–9   *galpinii*, 115
6–9   'Little Maid', 108, **116**
6–9   *macowanii*, 115
6–9   *nelsonii*, 115
6–9   *triangularis triangularis*, **115**
5–9   *uvaria*, 116

5–9   *Lathyrus vernus*, 46
4–8   *Leuzea centaurioides*, 49

5–9   *Ligularia dentata*, 49, 50
        'Desdemona', 49
        'Moorblüt', 49
        'Othello', 48, 49
5–9   'Gregynog Gold', **48**, 50
5–9   × *hessei*, 50
5–9   *macrophylla*, **49**, 50
      Lilium, 117–121
4–9   *candidum*, **117**
5–8   *centifolium*, **118**
3–8   *martagon*, 118, **119**, 120
4–7   *pyrenaicum*, 120
4–7   var. *rubrum*, **120**
4–7   'Shuksan', **120**, 121
4–8   *speciosum*, **121**
3–8   *Lobelia cardinalis*, 50
annual   *erinus*, 50
7–9   *fulgens*, 50
        'Queen Victoria', 50
5–8   *syphilitica*, 50
        'Eulalia Berridge', 50, **51**
6–9   *Lomelosia minoana*, **76**, 77
6–9   *Lunaria rediviva*, Honesty, Moonwort, 50–51
        'Alba', 50
        'Munstead Variety', 50
5–8   *Lychnis* × *arkwrightii*, **51**
5–8   × *haageana*, 51
5–9   *Lysichiton americanum*, **122**, 123
5–9   *camtschatcensis*, 123

      Maidenhair Fern. See *Adiantum*
7–9   *Malvastrum lateritium*, 51, **52**
      Matilija Poppy. See *Romneya coulteri*
      Matteuccia, 2
5–8   *orientalis*, 5
2–9   *struthiopteris*, Ostrich Plume Fern, 5
      Meconopsis, 52–55
      baileyi. See *M. betonicifolia*
6–8   *betonicifolia*, 52
6–8   *chelidonifolia*, 55
6–8   × *cookei*, **54**, 55
6–8   *grandis*, 52, 54
7–8   *punicea*, 54, 55
6–8   *quintuplinervia*, Harebell Poppy, **53**, 54, 55
7–8   × *sheldonii* 'Slieve Donard', 52, **53**
6–8   *villosa*, **55**
5–8   *Milium effusum* 'Aureum', **88**, 89
8–9   *Milligania densiflora*, **122**, 123

Monkshood. See *Aconitum napellus*
Moonwort. See *Lunaria rediviva*

Narcissus, 123–124
4–8   'Actaea', 10
6–9   *bulbocodium citrinus*, **123**
4–8   *cernuus* 'Plenus', 124
4–8   'Jana', **122**, 123
4–8   *moschatus* 'Plenus', 124
5–8   *poeticus recurvus*, 58
4–8   *pseudonarcissus*, 124, **154**
4–8   'Rijnveld's Early Sensation', 123
4–8   *Nepeta govaniana*, **56**
4–8   *nervosa*, 56, **57**
       Nipponanthemum nipponicum. See *Chrysanthemum nipponicum*
6–8   *Nomocharis pardanthina*, **124**

       Onion. See *Allium*
       Oreochome candollei. See *Selinum wallichianum*
       Osmunda, 6, 11
4–8   *cinnamomea*, **6**, 7
4–8   *claytoniana*, 7
4–9   *regalis*, Royal Fern, 2, 5, 7
          'Cristata', 7
          'Purpurascens', 7
       Ostrich Plume Fern. See *Matteuccia struthiopteris*
       Oxlip. See *Primula elatior*

       Paeonia, 58–61
4–8   *albiflora* 'Whitleyi Major', 61
5–8   *arietina*, **59**
          'Mother of Pearl', 58
3–8   'Avant Garde', 58, **60**
3–8   'Early Bird', 58
4–8   *lactiflora* 'The Bride', **61**
6–8   *lobata* 'Fire King', 58
3–9   *officinalis*, 57
6–8   *peregrina*, 58, **59**
6–8   *veitchii*, 58
6–8   var. *woodwardi*, **58**
5–7   *wittmanniana*, 58
       Pampas Grass. See *Cortaderia selloana*
8–11   *Pancratium illyricum*, 115
5–7   *Papaver atlanticum*, 61
4–9   *lateritium*, 61, **62**
5–9   *pilosum*, 61

6–9   *rupifragum*, 61
7–9   *Paradisea liliastrum*, St Bruno's Lily, **125**
8–10   *Parahebe perfoliata*, 62
       Pasque Flower. See *Pulsatilla vulgaris*
9–10   *Pelargonium*, 37
6–8   *Peltiphyllum peltatum*. See *Darmera peltata*
7–9   *Pennisetum orientale*, 89
4–7   *Persicaria* (*Polygonum*) *alpinum*, 64, 66
5–8   *amphibia*, 66, **67**
6–9   *vacciniifolium*, 66, **67**
4–8   *virginiana*, 66, **68**
          'Painter's Palette', 68
7–10   *Phlomis samia* var. *maroccana*, **63**
5–8   *Phuopsis stylosa*, 63, **64**
       Phygelius, Cape Figwort, 64
7–9   *aequalis*, 64
8–9   *capensis*, 64, **65**
          'Yellow Trumpet', 64, **65**
       Plagiorrhegma dubia. See *Jeffersonia dubia*
       Polygonum. See *Persicaria*
          amphibium, Willow Grass. See *Persicaria amphibia*
3–8   *Polystichum acrostichoides*, 7
5–8   *munitum*, Christmas Fern, **6**, 7
6–8   *polyblepharum*, **6**, 7
6–9   *squarrosum*, 7
       Primula, 69
5–7   'Devon Cream', **69**
4–8   *elatior*, Oxlip, 69
3–8   *veris*, Cowslip, 69
4–8   *Prunus avium* 'Plena', **146**
5–8   *Pulsatilla alpina apiifolia*, 68
4–9   *vulgaris*, Pasque Flower, 14, 68
9–10   *Puya alpestris*, 125, **126**

5–8   *Ranunculus aconitifolius* 'Flore Pleno', Fair Maids of France, 69, **70**
5–8   *constantinopolitanus* 'Plenus', **71**
8–9   *cortusoides*, 71
       gouanii. See *R. constantinopolitanus* 'Plenus'
4–8   *speciosus plenus*. See *R. constantinopolitanus* 'Plenus'
       Red Hot Poker. See *Kniphofia*
5–9   *Rheum officinale*, 71, **72**
       Rhubarb. See *Rheum officinale*
5–6   *Rodgersia aesculifolia*, 72
5–7   *pinnata* 'Superba', 72, **73**
5–7   *sambucifolia*, 72, **73**, 74

6–9   *Romneya coulteri*, California Tree Poppy, Matilija Poppy, 74–75

6–9   *trichocalyx* 'White Cloud', **74**, 75

5–8   *Salvia argentea*, **75**

4–7   *Sambucus*, 10, 72

5–7   *Saxifraga longifolia* 'Tumbling Waters', 76–77

4–7   *manschuriensis*, **76**

   peltata. See *Darmera peltata*

6–8   *Scabiosa (Lomelosia) minoana*, **76**, 77

6–9   *Schizostylis coccinea*, Kaffir Lily, 126

   'Sunrise', 126, **127**

   Scotch Flame Flower. See *Tropaeolum speciosum*

6–9   *Selinum wallichianum (S. tenuifolium)*, **77**

   Senecio clivorum. See *Ligularia dentata*

   ledebourii. See *Ligularia macrophylla*

   Skunk Cabbage. See *Symplocarpus foetidus*

4–9   *Smilacina racemosa*, 126, **127**

   Spiraea palmata. See *Filipendula palmata*

7–9   *Stenanthium robustum*, **128**

   Struthiopteris germanica. See *Matteuccia struthiopteris*

   Sweet Rocket. See *Hesperis matronalis*

3–9   *Symphytum asperum*, 78

3–9   *officinale*, Comfrey, 78

4–8   × *uplandicum* 'Variegatum', **78**

4–8   *Symplocarpus foetidus*, Skunk Cabbage, 121

   Tecoma. See *Campsis*

5–9   *Thalictrum diffusiflorum*, 78, **79**

4–9   *Thermopsis montana*, 79, **80**

4–8   *Tovara virginiana*. See *Persicaria virginiana*

   Tree fern. See *Dicksonia*

4–9   *Trillium erectum*, 128, **129**

4–9   *grandiflorum*, **130**, 131

   'Plenum', **129**

   'Roseum', **131**

7–9   *Tropaeolum speciosum*, 79

   Trumpet Vine. See *Campsis*

5–8   *Tulipa sprengeri*, 131, **132**

6–9   *Urospermum dalechampii*, **81**

9–10   *Ursinea sericea*, 81

4–9   *Uvularia grandiflora*, **132**, 133

5–8   *Veratrum album*, **133**

3–8   *nigrum*, **133**

3–8   *viride*, 133, **134**

   Veronica perfoliata. See *Parahebe perfoliata*

   White Helleborine. See *Veratrum album*

   Wood Anemone. See *Anemone nemorosa*

   Wormwood. See *Artemisia absinthium*

4–10   *Yucca filifera*, 134, **135**

   flaccida. See *Y. filifera*

   'Vittorio Emmanuele II', 134, **135**

8–10   *Zantedeschia aethiopica* 'Crowborough', **136**, 137

   Zauschneria. See *Epilobium canum*

3–9   *Zigadenus elegans*, **136**, 137

PHOTO CREDITS

My thanks to the friends who helped with photographs. Their contributions are on the following pages: John Elsley: 3, 4, 6 bottom, 8, 16 bottom, 18 top, 20 right, 22, 25, 27, 32 top, 36 bottom, 37, 40, 41, 42, 60, 63, 73 bottom, 74, 82, 87, 88, 90, 96, 98, 103, 104, 108, 109 top, 115, 116, 122 top, 127, 129 bottom, 130, 132 bottom; Pamela Harper: 13, 18 bottom, 20 left, 47, 70; Edward A. McRae: 118; Roger Raiche: 30 right; Hazel le Rougetel: 117; George Waters: 21, 31, 32 bottom, 65 bottom, 94, 105, 111 all, 138, 142. All other photographs are my own.

G.S.T.

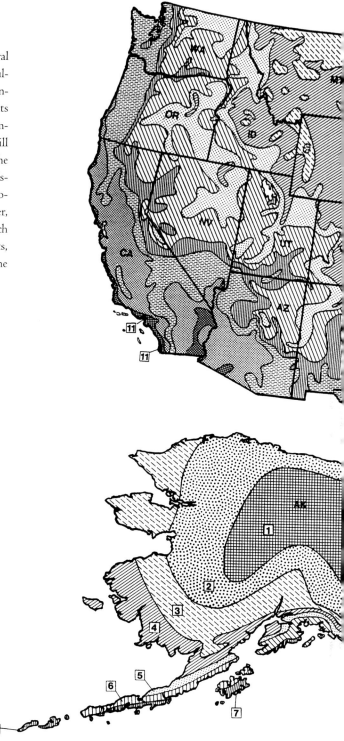

PLANT HARDINESS ZONES
IN THE UNITED STATES

This hardiness map was developed by the Agricultural Research Service of the U.S. Department of Agriculture. The hardiness zones are based on the average annual minimum temperature for each zone. All plants are designated with a number spread, the lower number indicating the most northerly area where they will reliably survive the winter, and the higher number the most southerly area where they will perform consistently. Many factors, such as altitude, degree of exposure to wind, proximity to bodies of water, snow cover, soil types and the like can create variations of as much as two zones in winter hardiness, while cool nights, shade and amount of water received can extend the southern limits.

See Index of Plants for zone listings.

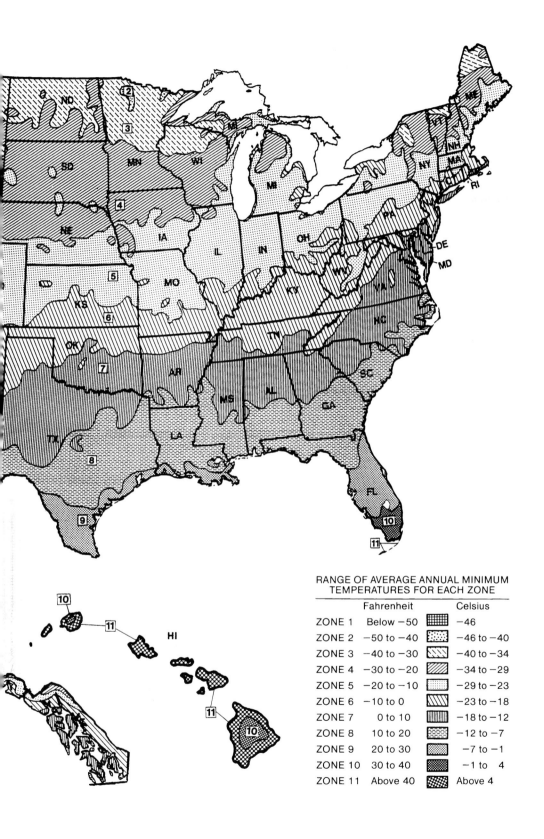

RANGE OF AVERAGE ANNUAL MINIMUM
TEMPERATURES FOR EACH ZONE

	Fahrenheit		Celsius
ZONE 1	Below −50		−46
ZONE 2	−50 to −40		−46 to −40
ZONE 3	−40 to −30		−40 to −34
ZONE 4	−30 to −20		−34 to −29
ZONE 5	−20 to −10		−29 to −23
ZONE 6	−10 to 0		−23 to −18
ZONE 7	0 to 10		−18 to −12
ZONE 8	10 to 20		−12 to −7
ZONE 9	20 to 30		−7 to −1
ZONE 10	30 to 40		−1 to 4
ZONE 11	Above 40		Above 4

Treasured Perennials, edited by George Waters and Melody Lacina,
was produced by Carol Lewis at Sagapress, Inc. John Elsley supplied information
on plant hardiness zones. Iron Horse Graphics, Ltd., designed the book. Jacket design
and book composition were done by Melissa Ehn at Wilsted & Taylor Publishing Services.
The roman text type is Centaur, designed by Bruce Rogers in 1914 for the Metropolitan Museum
of New York; he used it in the celebrated 1929 *Oxford Lectern Bible*. Arrighi, the italic text type,
was designed by Frederic Warde in 1925 to accompany the Monotype Corporation's cut of
Centaur. The display type is Titling Forum, designed by F. W. Goudy around 1912.
The book was printed by World Print, Ltd., in Hong Kong.